GROWING
VEGETABLES

D1428564

GROWING VEGETABLES

A step-by-step guide to planning, planting and produce

ALEX SMITH

ARCTURUS

ARCTURUS

This edition published in 2011 by Arcturus Publishing Limited
26/27 Bickels Yard, 151–153 Bermondsey Street,
London SE1 3HA

ISBN: 978-1-84837-752-3
AD001679EN

Printed in Singapore

The Fell Types are digitally reproduced by Igino Marini. www.iginomarini.com

CONTENTS

INTRODUCTION

In these days of anxieties about food miles and the use of pesticides in agriculture, growing your own food has become a hot topic. During the second half of the 20th century, with well-stocked supermarkets proliferating and the food shortages of the war years a fading memory, tending a vegetable patch was often regarded as a rather stuffy occupation for the middle-aged. Now, however, vegetable-growing has a revitalized image and people of all ages are interested in the most reliable way of knowing exactly where your food comes from – producing it yourself.

You don't need to have a large garden to grow some produce, and a vegetable patch doesn't have to mean dull rows of all-green plants. Companion planting, using flowers and herbs to improve the health of the vegetables, brings a decorative effect as well as fulfilling a practical purpose. Vegetables such as Swiss chard varieties can provide striking colour, and beans can be found now in several attractive shades. Thinking about the visual effects you can achieve as well as what you want to eat allows you to incorporate vegetables happily into your garden without setting aside a special area that is purely functional.

However, if space is limited it makes sense to grow produce that is unusual or expensive rather than, say, potatoes. If your garden is really small, 'square foot gardening', with a raised bed no larger than 1.5 sq m (16 sq ft), divided into squares and intensively planted, will allow you a surprising amount of scope. Make the most of vertical space, growing plants up canes, and cluster herbs in pots conveniently near the kitchen door.

GETTING AN ALLOTMENT

If you want to grow food on a larger scale than your garden allows, the answer is to get an allotment on land provided by your local council. Five or ten years ago there was only limited interest in allotments and many were untended and overgrown. In recent years, however, demand has soared and waiting lists are long – so it is important to consider the practicalities of having an allotment before you embark on what will probably be a time-consuming search. It is a major commitment of time and effort; on the other hand, it is a source of good exercise in the fresh air as well as providing a steady supply of home-grown food.

A simple search on the internet should give you a list of local sites and the telephone number of whom you should contact at your council. Alternatively, if you know the location of your nearest allotments, ask one of the plot holders how to make an application. Usually people are only too happy to help. You can also ask them about the site, what security arrangements there are and how fertile the land is.

While you may be on the waiting list for some time, you may eventually be given a choice of plots. Allotment holders change throughout the year; some find it too arduous as they get older, some lose interest, and a few may be excluded if they don't keep the plot to required standards. A plot may be left untended but not given up until it's time to renew the subscription. So, frequently, several plots become available at the same time.

If you are offered a plot that is smaller than you want, take it – at least you will get on to the site. A bigger plot will probably become free later and may be easier to lay hands on if you are already an allotment holder.

However, do not try to take on more than you can manage, as there are only so many hours in the day. A full-sized plot is 250 sq m (300 sq yd) – definitely too much for one person in terms of both cultivation and the ability to eat all the produce. Unless you have a family of helpers it is better to take a smaller plot or consider sharing; most sites now provide half-sized plots.

PRACTICAL CONSIDERATIONS

If you can acquire an allotment near your home, this will make things much easier when it comes to getting there and, especially, transporting materials. If you plan to cycle there, remember that it is very difficult carrying bags of fertilizer or bricks by bike, so access by other modes of transport will be needed occasionally.

Check the quality of the plot. A few thistles and nettles are relatively easy to remove and indicate a fertile soil, but thicker-rooted perennial weeds such as brambles are more difficult to get rid of and could involve a lot of hard digging work.

Even with a water butt to collect rainwater you may need to rely upon the site's water supply for irrigation, so consider the distance to the nearest access point – water is heavy to carry. Avoid sites with shady trees as most crops require good sunlight to thrive. Remember to take this into account if you are viewing the plot in winter – bare trees may be transformed into very leafy shade in summer. However, smaller hedges and bushes may be good windbreaks.

PART 1

STARTING A VEGETABLE PLOT

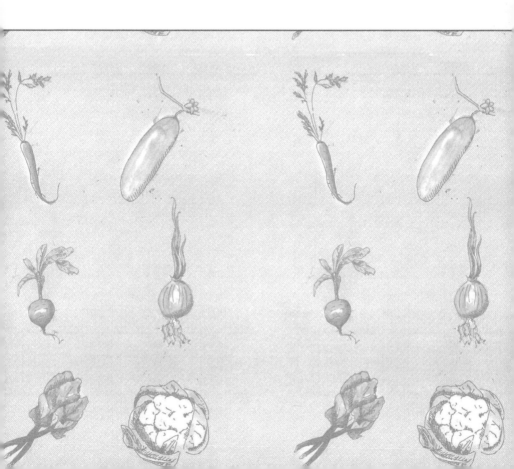

TOOLS

Tools are of course essential to managing a vegetable plot. They do not need to be expensive, but before buying check that they will be strong enough to do the job – some modern tools have a tendency to snap when the going gets tough. Looking around boot fairs for tools made in the old-fashioned way with wooden shafts worn smooth by constant usage can pay dividends. Here are some of the basic tools you will need:

Spade The essential tool for digging, so choose a good make with a sharp blade. Test it for size in the shop. Stainless steel blades are easy to clean but they are more expensive. Carbon steel spades are probably the strongest as they have no join between the blade and shaft; these are more easily found at a builder's merchant than a garden centre. Spades are not to be confused with shovels, which have raised edges for scooping up loose material.

Fork With four prongs, a fork sometimes penetrates the ground more easily than a spade and may be better for turning heavy or wet soil. It is also useful for lifting clumps of weeds as you can shake off the valuable topsoil before disposing of the weeds.

Hoes and rakes Although mainly intended for weeding, hoes can be used for aerating the soil and forming seed drills. A Dutch hoe has an angled head designed to slice through weeds. A rake is useful when levelling soil.

Hand fork This tool is great for weeding and taking out plants undamaged.

Hand trowel Buy the best and strongest you can afford, as they are always in use and are essential for digging small holes.

Dibber This pointed wooden stick is for making holes in the ground for seeds or small seedlings.

Secateurs These are in use all year round for cutting and pruning, so buy a good-quality stainless steel set as the cheaper ones tend to break easily.

Watering can Hoses are forbidden on many allotments and recent hot summers have also seen the introduction of blanket hose-pipe bans. Two watering cans may be best. Use strong plastic ones to lighten the load. Water is heavy – a full 9 litre (2 gal) watering can weighs about 8 kg (18 lb).

Water butt Catching rainwater saves both your energy and tap water. Raise it on blocks so you can get a watering can beneath the tap.

Compost bin See pages 14–15.

Wheelbarrow Essential for shifting large bags of manure or compost. It is best to buy a barrow from a builder's merchant as they are much stronger than garden centre plastic ones.

Twine and garden lines These are indispensable for tying up plants, marking out plots and so forth.

Gardening knife Essential for cutting and chopping anything from plants to string. Keep the blade dry and sharp.

Scissors These have many uses, not least for cutting salad leaves and herbs.

Pencil and tape measure For when you are designing or planning. Make sure the tape measure is a long one.

Scarecrow No one knows if they really scare the crows, but they are good fun and make a friend to chat to.

Boots Strong footwear is essential, as it is no good trying to dig a vegetable garden in trainers.

PREPARING THE GROUND

If you have a new allotment, the unfortunate truth is that you may arrive to find it overgrown and covered in weeds. There is no better way to get rid of weeds than to dig them out. Digging helps to aerate the soil, improves drainage and soil structure and gives you a chance to add manure or compost to your plot. Autumn and early winter are the best time for digging; all crops have been harvested and the soil is not too heavy and wet.

But don't go mad! You can't dig a whole allotment, or even a decent-sized vegetable plot in your own garden, in one session; 10–20 minutes at a time will be fine. Then have a cup of tea or do some gentle pottering. It pays to have a bit of a stretching routine before you start and straighten your back from time to time during the session. Digging is good exercise but be careful not to overdo the first session.

To dig properly, use a good-quality sharp spade and make two insertions, one at 90 degrees to the other, then lift and turn the soil. If the soil is inverted properly most annual weeds will be killed and will decompose in the soil. Remove the roots of perennial weeds by hand to prevent their spread.

There are two main types of digging – single and double. The difference is the depth that you dig. A single dig is a trench dug to the depth of one spade, while a double dig is twice as deep – two spade depths. Double digging is more effective for improving drainage as it breaks up the compacted soil below the surface – but, of course, it requires double the effort!

STEP-BY-STEP
DIGGING TECHNIQUE

1 Mark out the area to be dug with string and divide in two. Dig the first trench about 45 cm (18 in) wide.

2 Throw the soil in front of you, turning it upside down to expose roots. Pick out the weed roots. Mix some compost into the trench.

3 Dig out the next 45 cm (18 in) of soil, working backwards. Throw the soil on top of the compost in the previous trench. Remove weeds as you go.

4 Repeat with successive trenches around the area.

5 When you get to the end, fill in the last trench with the soil excavated from the first trench.

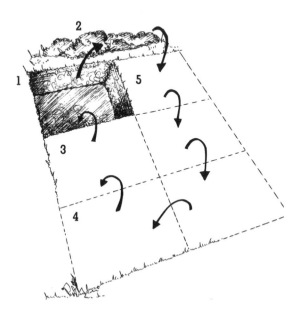

IMPROVING THE SOIL

For plants to flourish they need soil with good structure in which the required nutrients are not only present but active. All soil benefits from the addition of plenty of garden compost or rotted manure. Clay soils can be improved by adding lime. If you cannot dig more material into the soil, use plenty of organic surface mulches or chipped wood bark which will eventually degrade and be worked into the soil.

One of the first things you need to grow vegetables successfully is a **compost bin**. These are available from all DIY stores and garden centres, but you can also make your own. The key to making good compost is to keep the air circulating through the material. Use a bin as large as possible; this generates more heat and accelerates rotting.

Place twigs and cuttings at the bottom, then pile on kitchen and garden refuse. Do not use thick prunings unless they have been shredded first. A compost activator will speed up the rotting process by stimulating bacterial growth. Keep the material moist.

After a few weeks, put a fork through the compost and turn it, moving the material from the outside into the middle and vice versa. This will aerate the compost and help all the material to degrade evenly.

Liming is required on acidic soil to grow certain vegetables such as cabbages. Spread lime on top of the soil at any time of year but as far in advance of planting as possible. Mix it through with a spade. Do not add lime at the same time as compost as the two react against each other.

STEP-BY-STEP
MAKING A COMPOST BIN

1 Cut four wooden stakes of equal length. Whittle to a point at one end.

2 Hammer the stakes into the ground 1 m (3¼ ft) apart to form a square. Fix plastic netting around the stakes with nails.

3 Cut old cardboard into four pieces the size of each side. Line each side with the cardboard. Finally, load up the bin with your garden and kitchen refuse.

1

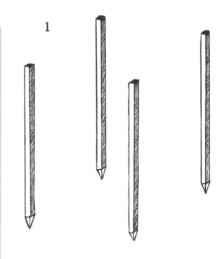

2

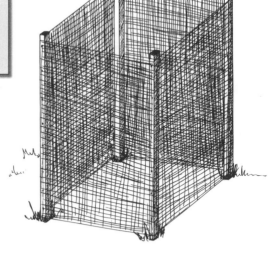

3

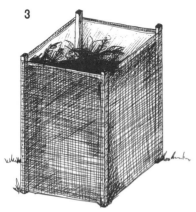

CROP ROTATION

By rotating the planting position of the various crops you are growing, you can help to prevent the build-up of pests and diseases. You can group together crops with similar needs in terms of soil fertility and pH levels and move them around so that they do not grow in the same spot for at least another three years. By changing the crops every year you will minimize overuse of the soil and allow it to replenish itself. The soil structure will also be improved by alternating deep-rooted and fibrous-rooted crops.

There are several variations on crop rotation, but in a decent-sized garden or an allotment, the three-year rotation cycle shown here would be appropriate.

GROUP A
Aubergines, beetroot, carrots, celery, celeriac, courgettes, cucumbers, garlic, leeks, marrows, onions, parsnips, peppers, potatoes, pumpkins, salsify, shallots, tomatoes.

GROUP B
Broad beans, chicory, endive, French beans, lettuce, peas, runner beans, spinach, sweetcorn.

GROUP C
Broccoli, brussels sprouts, cabbages, cauliflowers, kale, kohlrabi, turnips, radishes, swedes.

GROUP D
Any crops that need to remain undisturbed in the same place: asparagus, currants, globe artichokes, gooseberries, rhubarb.

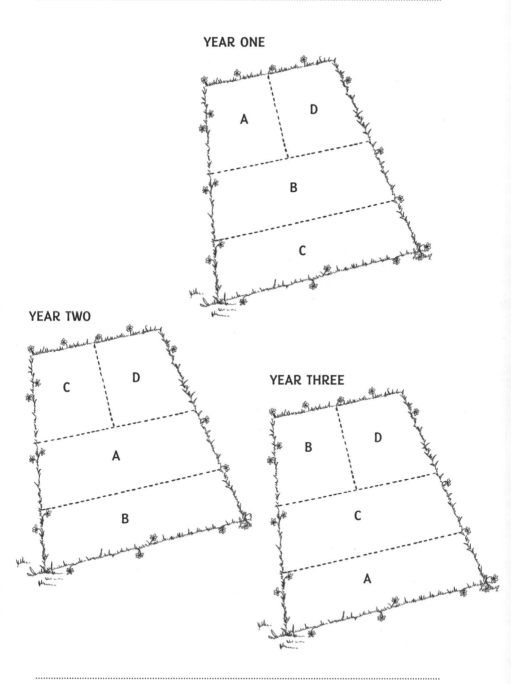

YEAR ONE

YEAR TWO

YEAR THREE

SOIL pH LEVELS AND WATERING

The pH value of the soil tells you how acidic or alkaline it is. Simple and inexpensive soil-testing kits are available which will give you a quick result without the expense of a proper laboratory test. Some plants prefer slightly acidic conditions while others prefer alkaline – for example, potatoes can suffer more from blight in alkaline soils, whereas brassicas prefer them. However, so long as the pH is not too extreme most plants will thrive.

The pH scale runs from 1 (very acidic) to 14 (very alkaline). Most soil is between 4 and 8. The presence of calcium from chalk, found especially in the south of England, makes the soil slightly alkaline with a pH of around 8. One common indicator of soil pH is the hydrangea; the flowers are pink in chalky alkaline soil but blue in acidic soil.

Here is a general analysis of different soil types:

pH 4 Upland peat
pH 5 Pine forest and heaths
pH 6 Deciduous forests
pH 7 Farmland and fens
pH 8 Chalk and limestone

Some common fruit and vegetable preferences for acid or alkaline soil are:

Acidic Blueberries, carrots, citrus fruits, cranberries, endives, potatoes, radishes, rhubarb, strawberries.

Alkaline Asparagus, beetroot, Brussel sprouts, broccoli, cauliflower, grapes, leeks, onions, shallots.

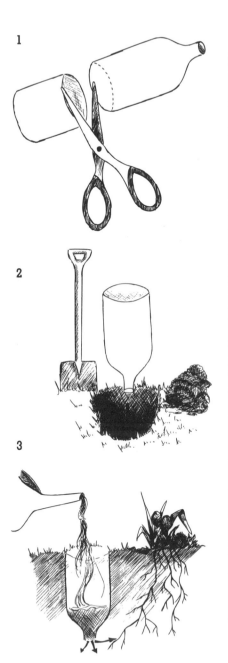

1

2

3

A WATERY TIP

Water is as essential to plant life as it is to human life. In dry seasons you must water your crops or they will die. Do not water at noon or the hot mid afternoon; early morning or late evening is best, so that the water has time to sink into the ground before evaporating in the heat. Beware of excessive watering, though, as this will inhibit the development of a strong root system.

For some particularly thirsty plants such as marrows and other squashes it is often a good idea to cut off the bottom of a plastic bottle and stick the bottle upside down 15 cm (6 in) deep into the soil beside the plant. You can then pour water into the bottle and it goes straight down to the roots rather than lying on the surface (see diagrams left).

SHEDS, TOOL STORES, GREENHOUSES AND COLD FRAMES

Unfortunately, many allotments don't allow sheds as they can cast shade over other plots. Check your lease for shed restrictions; if sheds are allowed on your plot, aim to get one as you will find it very useful indeed.

If sheds are not allowed, the next best thing is a tool store. They come in all shapes, sizes and prices, but generally a sturdy plastic one should suffice.

A greenhouse at home or on your plot will extend your growing season, but before getting one for an allotment do consult the site rules. If you cannot have a greenhouse, a cold frame is essential for germinating seeds and protecting young plants. Follow these simple instructions to make your own.

STEP-BY-STEP MAKING A COLD FRAME

A cold frame can be made from old pallet wood, but it is assumed here you are buying new timber.

YOU WILL NEED:

6 × 120 cm (4 ft) of 15 × 2.5 cm (6 × 1 in) timber planks for the base.

250 cm (8 ft) of 5 × 2.5 cm (2 × 1 in) timber batten for joining the base planks.

120 cm (4 ft) wooden dowel for the corner joints of the base.

12 galvanized screw eyes (to fit the dowel) for the corner joints.

4 × 120 cm (4 ft) of 10 × 2.5 cm (4 × 1 in) timber planks for the lid.

120 × 120 cm (4 × 4 ft) plastic sheeting for the lid.

2 hinges for the lid

1 carriage bolt and wing nut.

Screws and nails.

Saw, screwdriver and hammer.

METHOD:

1 Use the six 15 × 2.5 cm (6 × 1 in) timber planks to make the base. Four planks make the box for the base, one plank goes on top at the back. The last plank is cut diagonally for the angled sides. Draw a diagonal line from one corner to the opposite corner and saw down the line.

2 Fix each diagonal piece to the base sides by nailing through the pieces of 5 × 2.5 cm (2 × 1 in) timber batten. Join the two back boards together in the same way.

3 Each corner is joined together by using galvanized screw eyes and wooden dowels. Alternate the screw eyes in the corners and slip in the dowels. This design means you can take the frame apart easily should you want to move it.

4 Build the lid using the four 10 × 2.5 cm (4 × 1 in) timber planks. Cut the side pieces at an angle by lining up a straight edge with the frame below. Nail together.

5 Attach the lid to the frame using the hinges then nail the plastic to the top. Attach a 5 × 2.5 cm (2 × 1 in) timber batten to the front with a carriage bolt and wing nut. Use the batten to hold the lid open to vent the frame when necessary.

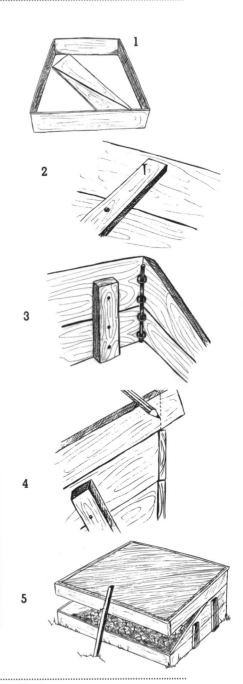

STAKING AND SUPPORTING

Good supports will be almost unnoticed once the plants have grown, yet they can make all the difference to a whole range of plants, including runner beans, French beans, peas and even tomatoes. Choose appropriate supports and insert them in the soil while the plants are still small.

The crossed canes method of support is useful for runner beans and peas. Insert the canes in angled pairs then slide a horizontal cane along the V formed at the top. Push the cane down until all the angled pairs are secure then tie to prevent sideways movement.

A wigwam of canes can be used at the back of a border for climbers and scramblers such as runner beans or peas. See opposite for how to make a wigwam.

Plastic wigwam cane holders are quick and easy to use – see (2) opposite. Plastic-coated metal supports are more expensive to buy but will last for years. Nylon netting stretched between two stout posts is a good support for both peas and beans. Use 10 cm (4 in) mesh and tie it on securely. You may have to thread young beans through to give them a start. Remember that the net will offer a lot of wind resistance when covered with foliage.

Individual canes are very useful for plants such as tomatoes, but make sure enough cane is pushed into the ground, otherwise it will not support the weight of a fully fruiting plant.

MAKING A WIGWAM OF CANES

1 Tie about 4–6 canes together close to the top so they form a wigwam. This is ideal for just a few beans.

2 A wigwam cane holder is a quick alternative. It will hold the canes firmly and well spaced for an attractive wigwam.

3 Runner beans will twine themselves around the canes with a little help from you.

4 For a whole row, insert two rows of canes at a slight angle so they cross near the top.

5 Slide a horizontal cane along the top in the V formed by the crossed canes and pull it down firmly. Tie them all together to prevent movement.

6 If the row is long, you will need to insert another cane and overlap the two.

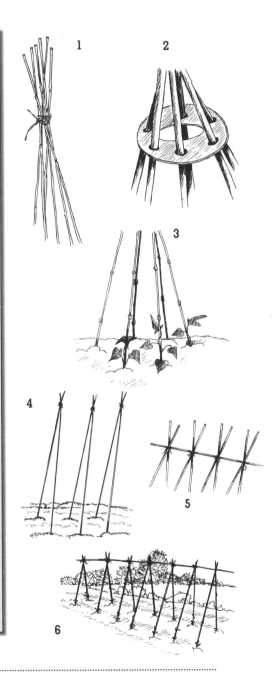

COMPANION PLANTING

When planning the layout of your crops, it is a good idea to allow space for companion plants that will repel pests or act as a decoy – for example, the smell of leeks can deter the carrot fly from attacking carrots. Some companion plants can also improve flavour and growth. The table on these two pages lists the companions that are good for each other.

VEGETABLE	LIKES	DISLIKES
Asparagus	Basil, tomato, parsley, nasturtium	Onion, garlic, potato
Aubergine	Beans, pepper, potato, spinach	
Beans	Carrot, cabbage, cucumber, cauliflower, marigold	Chives, leek, garlic
Broad bean	Brassicas, carrot, celery, corn, lettuce, potato	Fennel
Beetroot	Brassicas, lettuce, onion, sage	Beans
Broccoli	Celery, chamomile, dill, rosemary	Oregano, strawberry
Brussels sprout	Potato, thyme	Strawberry
Cabbage	Beetroot, potato, oregano, sage	Strawberry, tomato
Carrot	Beans, lettuce, onion, peas, radish, tomato	Chives, dill, parsnip

VEGETABLE	LIKES	DISLIKES
Cauliflower	Beans, celery, oregano	Nasturtium, peas, potato, strawberry, tomato
Celery	Cabbage, leek, onion, spinach, tomato	Parsnip, potato
Corn	Beans, cucumber, melon, peas, pumpkin, potato, radish	Tomato
Courgette	Nasturtium	
Cucumber	Beans, celery, lettuce, peas, radish	Cauliflower, potato, basil
Leek	Carrot, celery, strawberry	
Lettuce	Carrot, radish, strawberry	Beans, beetroot, parsley
Melon	Corn, radish	Potato
Onion	Broccoli, cabbage, lettuce, strawberry, tomato	Beans, peas
Peas	Beans, carrot, sweetcorn, cucumber, radish	Onion family
Potato	Beans, sweetcorn, cabbage, peas, aubergine	Cucumber, pumpkin, squash, sunflower
Pumpkin	Corn	Potato
Spinach	Celery, cauliflower, aubergine	
Tomato	Asparagus, celery, carrot, parsley, marigold	Sweetcorn, fennel, potato

MAKING A BRICK PATH

A brick path can give a sturdy, structured look to a vegetable patch or allotment which is pleasant and also practical. A path such as this can be left for years but can also be moved easily if you want to rearrange the layout.

STEP-BY-STEP
MAKING A BRICK PATH

Collect old unbroken bricks wherever you can (skips and dumps). Lay them side-by-side to form the way you want your path to go.

1 Dig a shallow trench about two-thirds of a brick depth.

2 Lay the bricks in the trench with a 1 cm (½ in) gap between each. Stamp in with your foot. Scatter soil from the trench over the bricks and scrape into the cracks. Sweep clean.

3 Walk and wheelbarrow on the bricks to bed them down.

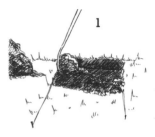

PART 2

WEEK-BY-WEEK CULTIVATION CALENDAR

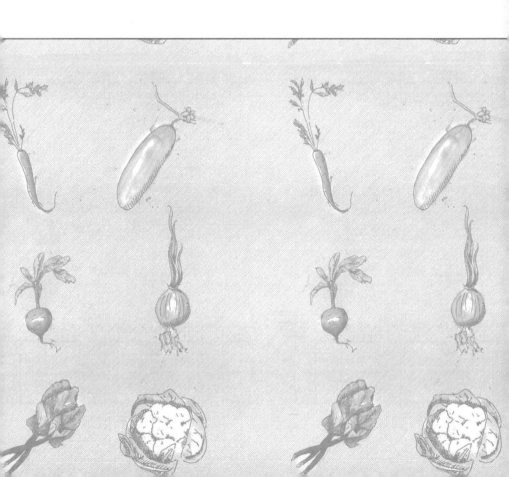

JANUARY INTRODUCTION

January is usually associated with hard frosts and cold north winds. If this isn't your first season for vegetable gardening and the forecast is for a period of frosty weather, dig up any remaining root crops such as swedes and parsnips and store them to prevent them freezing in the ground. If you want to do some January planting, sets of shallots and rhubarb crowns can go into the ground.

TEARJERKERS

Onions contain amino acid sulphoxides which form a sulphur compound when the onions are cut. This irritates the cornea of the eye, stimulating the lachrymal glands to produce tears to wash the irritant away.

THE ONION FAMILY

Onions have been used as food since Egyptian and Roman times and today they are grown on just about every allotment. They belong to a large family of plants, the Alliaceae. Commonly known as alliums, they all have a characteristically strong smell and many of them are essential ingredients in cookery worldwide.

The well-known family members include onions, garlic, shallots, leeks and chives. Many have recognized health benefits. Both onions and garlic have been shown to lower cholesterol levels and blood pressure. Allegedly, onions are also good for brainpower – experts are said to know their onions.

JANUARY
Week 1

This is a good month to flick through a few seed catalogues and make some sketches of what you are going to plant where in the coming year. Make use of your greenhouse to sow cauliflower seeds for a summer harvest. If the weather is mild you could also sow some aubergine and pepper seeds under glass.

SOWING AUBERGINES UNDER GLASS

Also known as eggplants, aubergines are from the Mediterranean and prefer warmer weather than we have in the UK. Sow them indoors or in the greenhouse to protect them from the cold and make the most of any sun that does peep through in January.

Prepare a seed tray with some potting compost and use a screw as a mini-dibber to make 3 mm ($1/8$ in) holes at 5 cm (2 in) intervals. The seeds are so small it may be best to use tweezers to put them in the holes if you have big fingers. Rake a light covering of soil over the seeds with your mini-dibber and lightly sprinkle with water. If your greenhouse is not heated, bring the seed tray back into the house for safekeeping and place on a sunny windowsill or in a porch until the plants are established. Move them into the greenhouse around mid-April or to a sheltered, sunny spot in the vegetable bed. They should be ready to pick in late summer.

AUBERGINE SNACK ATTACK

Simply slice thinly and flash fry in olive oil. Add a pinch of salt to provide a delicious aubergine snack.

JANUARY
Weeks 2&3

If you get a couple of sunny days, it is worth carefully emptying out any stored potato sacks to check for any rot. Discard any spoiled specimens. Tidy up sheds and greenhouses in preparation for spring. It is a good time to heel in your leeks.

THE WELSH LEEK

Leeks are big in Wales – in fact, the leek is the national vegetable. The daffodil, the other well-known symbol of Wales, is known in Welsh as *cenhenin Pedr* – St Peter's leek.

HEELING IN LEEKS

Winter crops such as leeks can occupy much-needed springtime planting space in the vegetable bed. Moving them to a different location is a good idea to free up space for planting new crops.

To do this, lift the leeks with a fork by levering them gently from beneath. Keep as much soil as possible around the roots when you pull them out. Transfer the leeks to a new position in freshly dug soil, placing them tightly together and packing soil round their roots.

They will happily stand 'heeled in' for weeks until you are ready to eat them.

JANUARY
Weeks 4&5

The breeding season for some garden birds is already under way and now is a good time to put up a bird box. Position it so as to maintain a fairly constant temperature, sheltered from direct sunlight and prevailing winds and rain. Protect the box from the local cats, the birds' main predator, by siting it well away from any perches or nearby branches strong enough to support a cat's weight. Cats can be very resourceful, so keep an eye out in case they have found a route you need to block.

RED RED ROBIN

Robins bob and weave around the garden at this time of year. The ground is often hard, so while you are digging they will take the chance to forage for insects in the freshly turned soil. Aggressive towards each other, they very soon become bold in the presence of a human who is a source of food.

FEBRUARY INTRODUCTION

Spring is coming and daffodils and crocuses are pushing up their green tips. The birds can feel it too and they are more active than before as the long winter nights recede. If the weather is kind you can begin sowing outdoors. Make a start with early peas and, towards the end of the month, with broad beans. Clean up your tools and wash out pots, baskets and trugs in readiness for a busy spring.

SUSSEX TRUGS

Trugs are traditional wooden garden baskets which have been made in Sussex for at least 200 years. The word 'trug' is derived from 'trog', an Anglo-Saxon word meaning boat-shaped wooden vessel. Originally used as measures or scoops for grain, trugs are still hand-made in Sussex today from willow and chestnut strips. They are especially useful around an allotment.

FEBRUARY
Week 1

Tidy up old mushy leaves from cabbages and Brussels sprouts and remove them to the compost heap. Watch out for the first crocuses and for frogs gathering in ponds to breed.

Jerusalem artichokes can be planted, as can shallots. Clear up and renew pathways, making them wide enough for comfortable wheelbarrow access.

THE INGENIOUS WHEELBARROW

Nobody knows who invented the wheelbarrow. The Chinese used primitive two-wheeled carts as early as the 1st century, but it wasn't until the 13th century AD that a one-wheeled barrow was in frequent use. The single wheel makes a wheelbarrow easy to manoeuvre along the narrow paths often found in gardens and allotments. It is an invaluable accessory for the allotment gardener in particular.

WHEELBARROW OR TROLLEY?

If a barrow has two wheels then it is a trolley and not a wheelbarrow.

FEBRUARY
Week 2

If you have a greenhouse, you could sow an early crop of lettuce, rocket and radish in seed trays.

If you would like an early crop of rhubarb now would be a good time to 'force' it. Cover the dormant crown with a bin insulated inside with straw or compost. This keeps the heat in and persuades the rhubarb stalks to put on a growth spurt. This will bring out sweet pink stems in April.

Listen out for the song of the thrush during February.

SONG THRUSHES

Song thrushes are similar to female blackbirds but slightly smaller, with brown spots on a pale chest. Their song is distinguished from that of a blackbird by its repeated phrases. They sing with their beaks wide open, turning their heads so that the listener gets the full effect of their echoing music. Thrushes have a varied diet – slugs, snails, insects, worms, berries and fruits. About a quarter of all song thrushes in the UK nest in back gardens and allotments.

SLUG PELLETS

Don't put down slug pellets as they can poison the thrushes when they eat the dead slugs. See page 43 for other ways to deter slugs.

FEBRUARY
Week 3

THE BRASSICAS

The Brassicaceae family encompasses a number of plants that have been among the mainstays of vegetable gardens for centuries. Many are hardy enough to grow through the winter. The term 'brassica' usually refers to cabbages, turnips, Brussels sprouts, kale, kohlrabi, broccoli, swedes and cauliflowers, though the family also includes rocket, radishes, cress and mustard as well as several non-vegetable plants such as oil-seed rape, alyssum and honesty. Brassicas can be found all over the world, although most genera grow in the northern temperate region.

Pathways can be created in February, ready to take the brunt of the springtime traffic. Make sure they are wide and accessible, since narrow paths can be exasperating to negotiate. Concrete paths are hard-wearing, but are too permanent for use in an allotment. Grass paths are suitable but do require regular mowing. Brick paths can be laid easily and rerouted with a minimum of fuss (see page 26), while wooden planks are perfect for affording temporary access. They protect the soil from getting too compacted and you from becoming too muddy.

If the weather is warm you can now sow some of your early brassicas under cloches – summer cabbages as well as turnips.

FEBRUARY
Week 4

Dig trenches for planting potatoes and add compost to the trenches. Prepare the ground for sowing peas. If weather permits, sow some *Calendula officinalis* seeds (pot marigolds). They grow to about 45 cm (18 in) high and have bright orange daisy-like flowers. Bees love them, and both the flowers and leaves can be eaten in salads. Plan out where to grow your gourds this year.

THE GOURDS

Gourds belong to a large family of plants known as Cucurbitaceae which includes cucumbers, courgettes, marrows, melons, squashes and pumpkins. They usually have yellow trumpet-shaped flowers.

Gourds grow at a fantastic rate, producing big plants just a few days after the seeds are sown. There are only a few edible types – most are used as implements, bowls, musical instruments, pipes and many other household objects.

ANCIENT SEEDS

Traces of gourd seeds that are over 7,000 years old have been found in Mexico.

MARCH INTRODUCTION

March is a month most gardeners look forward to. Spirits start to lift. Spring is in the air and animals, insects, plants and humans alike are stirred into activity by the impending approach of the new season. Onions and shallots can be planted outdoors in sets, and at the end of the month your first early potatoes can go into the ground.

COMPOST

Remember to turn your compost heap now. Remove any coarse mulch from the ground and add to the compost.

CROPS TO SOW

Beetroot

Broad beans

Brussels sprouts

Cabbage

Calabrese

Carrots

Celeriac

Endives

Kohlrabi

Leeks

Lettuce

Parsnips

Peas (early)

Radish

Spring onions

Turnips

MARCH
Week 1

BLACKBIRDS

Blackbirds foraging on the ground are a common sight in gardens and allotments, often turning over leaf litter to find grubs underneath. Blackbirds are members of the thrush family. The glossy black males have bright yellow beaks, while females are dull brown. They like to hunt worms early in the morning and last thing at night. Weeding usually brings them out in a hurry, bobbing and darting over the ground looking for freshly exposed worms. Blackbirds love berries, so growing shrubs with berries will encourage them to come to your garden or plot, where they will help to keep pests down – though you will have to sacrifice some fruit.

Using a sunny windowsill or the greenhouse, sow tomatoes, peppers, chillies, aubergines and cucumbers. Outside, you can sow beetroot, summer cabbages and early carrots under cloches. If you have enough space, put in some young fruit bushes and water generously with a bucketful of water for each plant. Keep well watered until they are well established. The fruit bushes will attract several types of birds.

MARCH
Week 2

The last of the leeks should now be dug up and parsnips should be pulled before the ground gets too warm. Clear spent kale leaves to the compost heap. Have a good sorting out and tidying up session in the shed, if you have one. Any badgers in the neighbourhood will be raising cubs born in February. Watch out for signs of them rooting around in an allotment.

BADGERS' RIGHT OF WAY

Badgers are busy in March, habitually using the same favourite paths on their evening foraging runs. Blocking their way with a fence can be a thankless task and just lead to a broken fence. There is no denying they can do a lot of damage to a vegetable plot. They are omnivorous members of the weasel family, eating earthworms, insects and grubs as well as amphibians, birds, roots and fruit. They are particularly partial to carrots, parsnips and potatoes. Growing your root veg in old raised-up oil drums filled with earth can be an effective defence. An old-timer's tip is that dousing the plot with human urine from a spray can also deter badgers.

BOOZY BADGERS

Badgers sometimes get drunk after eating rotting fruit, because the sugars released in the rotting process turn to alcohol.

MARCH
Week 3

It's time to start planning your regime for deterring and terminating pests. Try to avoid pesticides that remove the pests but also damage the wildlife. Spray aphids with a mixture of washing up liquid and water. This does not harm the natural predators such as ladybirds who will munch their way through the aphid population for you. Encourage frogs and toads – the natural slug and snail terminators – by creating a wildlife pond. Do not put goldfish in the pond, though, as they eat the tadpoles. Listen out for the first distinctive springtime knockings of the woodpeckers.

WOODPECKERS

The constant tree tapping of woodpeckers is a sure sign that spring is just around the corner. Great spotted woodpeckers are bigger than their blackbird-sized cousins the lesser spotted, but both have striking black-and-white feathers with red crowns. The great spotted makes a deep, resonant tapping, while the lesser spotted tends to nest and feed higher up and is quieter in its tapping. Their drumming is made by rapid blows of their beaks on tree trunks and branches. Inside their heads, woodpeckers have a series of little shock absorbers which cushion the blows and allow them to peck at up to ten drums a second. They also have zygodactyl feet – two toes pointing forward and two toes pointing backwards – providing an anchored stance when they peck.

MARCH
Week 4

Think about planting out strawberries around now. Remove the flowers during the first year to conserve the plants' energies and give yourself a bumper crop in year two. They reach their peak in year three and should be rotated in year four. Plant your first early potatoes; water your broad beans, rhubarb and onions well if the weather is dry. Keep busy with the hoe; pull out any remaining brassica plants and consign them to the compost heap. Keep an eye on the greenhouse tomatoes.

TOMATOES AND POTATOES

Have you ever noticed how similar the plants of the tomato and potato are? That is because they are closely related, both being members of the same family – Solanaceae. The family is probably the most widely cultivated in the UK. There are over 2,500 species – as well as tomatoes and potatoes, the family includes aubergines, peppers and herbs and flowers such as *Atropa belladonna* (deadly nightshade) and *Nicotiana* (tobacco).

THE MANDRAKE

Legend has it that mandrake, a famous member of the Solanaceae family, has magical powers. It features in Shakespeare, John Donne's poetry and Harry Potter. Every part of the plant is poisonous.

APRIL INTRODUCTION

April is the gardener's favourite month. The soil starts to warm up and the worst weather has long gone. The evenings are getting longer and lighter. However, there may still be the occasional frosty night so watch the weather forecast. It is a bit of a gap month between last year's late harvest and the new year's early crops, but there is a long list of crops to sow.

CROPS TO SOW

Aubergine, beetroot, broad beans, broccoli, Brussels sprouts, cabbage, calabrese, carrots, celery, cauliflower, chard, endives, kale, kohlrabi, leeks, lettuce, peas, radish, rocket, salsify, spinach, spring onions, turnips.

CARROTS, PARSNIPS AND CELERY

The frothy green foliage of carrots and parsnips is a major clue that these two plants are related before you even compare their roots. However, many other plants that are less obviously similar have this distinctive foliage too – it is a family trait of the Apiaceae, or Umbelliferae, a large group of plants commonly known as the celery family. As well as carrots and parsnips, other well-known cousins are celery, celeriac, fennel and parsley, along with weeds such as cow parsley and hogweed. Most of the family are aromatic and have hollow stems; some are poisonous, notably hemlock.

APRIL
Week 1

Slugs and snails are the gardener's number one enemy and they start to appear in abundance in April. Be ready to go to war, since they can decimate your crops overnight.

Slug pellets are effective but they also kill the animals that eat the slugs, so they are best avoided. Salt terminates slugs and snails efficiently and is kinder to the animals further up the food chain. Encourage slug and snail predators into your garden or allotment – frogs and toads, thrushes, hedgehogs and centipedes all love a slug.

Many gardeners set beer traps to attract slugs and drown them in alcohol. Blocking their slimy path across your plot with a barrier can also be effective, but rain does wash barriers away and so they need constant attention. Barrier examples that work include coffee, soot, ash, lime, sand, shingle, shredded wood bark, crushed eggshells and sawdust. Plants such as lavender, thyme, sage, geraniums and mint are also known to repel slugs and snails, so it is worth planting these round vulnerable crops.

THE CUCKOO

April is the month to listen out for the arrival for the cuckoo. This bird returns to Britain from Africa to breed each spring. After mating the female lays her eggs in other birds' nests – up to a dozen of them – where her young will hatch and push the other nestlings out. It is the male, however, that makes that distinctive cuc-koo call.

APRIL
Week 2

Patrol for slugs and snails at night with a torch – by 10 pm they will be out and about. Check your beer traps if you have set them.

Run a health check on all your crops. Sow some early and late purple sprouting broccoli. Young kale and Brussels sprouts plants can be put outside in the day, but remember to bring them in again at night as it is still chilly. There is a lot of growing being done in April and the wildlife residents are on the go too. Without too much protective foliage to hide them from view their activities can be fraught with danger. Sometimes kestrels and sparrowhawks are spotted around allotments preying on the birds and small creatures who live there.

BIRDS OF PREY

Birds of prey can be hard to tell apart, mainly because we only glimpse them at a distance. Kestrels can often be seen hovering over allotments, diving to eat their prey on the ground. The similar-looking hobby, on the other hand, can't hover at all and eats on the wing, catching insects mid-flight. Sparrowhawks have short wings and a long tail, distinguishing them from peregrine falcons, which have long wings and a short tail. Merlins are the smallest of the British birds of prey.

APRIL
Week 3

If the weather is clement move the tomato and pepper plants outside from the greenhouse to a sheltered position. Erect runner bean poles and wigwams. Be vigilant for slugs and snails with night patrols. Keep the hoe busy, weeding and clearing open ground in readiness for planting. Be prepared to bring plants in or cover them in case of frosts. Easter is a traditional time to be planting potatoes, including sweet potatoes. If there are bushes and trees nearby, you can probably enjoy watching birds building their nests.

NESTING BLUE TITS

Blue tit pairs are very active right now and are frequent visitors to gardens and allotments. They are agile little birds which are quick to exploit new food sources, and while many people put out bird feeders for the pleasure of watching them, the gardener can also gain practical value in encouraging their presence. If you have a tree in or bordering your garden or plot, putting up a nest box will soon result in the arrival of a breeding pair and their constant swoops from the nest box straight on to the pests on your plants will gladden your heart while you are tending your vegetables.

FOOD FOR BLUE TITS

Blue tits feed on caterpillars, aphids and other insects. The more yellow-green caterpillars a male bird eats, the brighter the yellow of his breast becomes.

APRIL
Week 4

Keep up the night patrols for slugs and check your beer traps. If there isn't much rain, make sure you give everything a bit of a drink to avoid the roots drying out. At the same time, keep an eye on the weather forecast for late frosts in case you need to cover up vulnerable seedlings in a hurry. Keep the hoe busy and clear open ground in preparation for planting. Work hard on carefully clearing perennial weeds.

A TOUCH OF LATEX

During World War II, dandelions were cultivated for the latex which was extracted from the root. This latex was used to make rubber.

PERENNIAL WEEDS, DANDELIONS AND DAISIES

Perennial weeds return year after year. Slower growing than other types of weed, species such as the dandelion survive the winter and summer through their water-retaining roots which also hold essential nutrients.

The daisy, so often found side-by-side with the dandelion, is a perennial flower that also retains winter moisture in its roots. The daisy's cheerful white flowers, often tinged with a little pink, are pretty as a picture alongside the yellow dandelions, brightening up the roadside and parks and heralding the coming of summer.

MAY INTRODUCTION

May is probably the busiest month for the vegetable gardener. Depending on where you live, you may already have some salad crops, spring onions and rhubarb to harvest. The two main jobs you need to keep on top of this month are hoeing and thinning out growing crops to give them plenty of room. There are lots of crops to sow this month, and it is worth planting staggered sets – plant one set then a few weeks later plant another set of the same crop so you get a succession of harvests. Keep an eye out for returning house martins.

THE HOUSE MARTIN RETURNS

House martins return to the UK to breed in the summer. They are a familiar sight in villages and towns, building their cup-shaped mud nests on the sides of buildings. They are similar in shape to swallows but with a shorter forked tail. Adults fly at high speed, catching insects on the wing. They are a migratory species, leaving for Africa in October and returning to Europe in April and May.

CROPS TO SOW

Broad beans, French beans, runner beans, beetroot, broccoli, cabbage, calabrese, carrots, cauliflower, chicory, endive, kale, kohlrabi, lettuce, peas, radish, salsify, spring onions, swedes, sweetcorn, turnips.

MAY
Week 1

Now would be good time to consider planting edible flowers if you haven't already. Some flowers are harmful to eat, but many are surprisingly delicious. While you may not have thought of it as a flower, the globe artichoke is in fact an unopened thistle bud. Nasturtium flowers are brightly coloured with a strong, peppery flavour, making them ideal for salads and pasta dishes. The compact, purple flower heads of chives have a slight onion flavour and can also be used in salads.

Once you have done your planting, reward yourself with some time out spent watching the swooping of the swallows around the garden or allotment.

SWALLOWS

Swallows are astonishingly agile in flight, darting and swerving as they catch insects on the wing. They can arrive from South Africa as early as March, hence the saying 'one swallow doesn't make a summer'. They are glossy blue-black with cream underparts and long tails; the male's red throat makes them easily distinguishable from swifts or house martins.

MAY
Week 2

CELERIAC

This vegetable does not promise much from its dull-coloured, knobbly appearance but is in fact tasty to eat. The surface is too uneven to peel like a potato, so just cut it away. Cut the flesh into the shapes you want and then immediately put the pieces into water acidulated with lemon juice or vinegar to prevent them from discolouring.

Celeriac mash is a fashionable way to cook this underrated vegetable, but you can also roast it, use it in soups or slice it raw into salads.

If your seedlings have made enough progress you can now begin to plant out Brussels sprouts, summer cabbages, celery and celeriac.

Tie in outdoor tomatoes to supporting canes and pinch out growth. Put supports around broad beans.

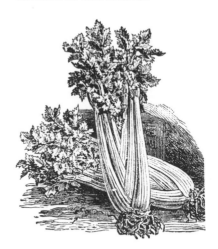

MAY
Week 3

Check the state of the whole vegetable patch. Do a health run-down of all the crops, removing pests and treating diseases. Hoe any open ground and between rows of veg to keep weeds at bay. Hand-weed potatoes. Sow spring onions and beetroot. Water swedes and turnips. Mow any grass paths and sweep brick or concrete paths. If you have any nettle patches, leave a few in situ to encourage ladybirds, which eat vast numbers of aphids.

DOCK LEAF MYTH

The broad-leaved dock that often grows alongside nettles has no sting-curing properties of any kind. The effect is illusory – the truth is that most nettle stings are mild and the pain fades quickly.

THE STINGING NETTLE

Nettles thrive in allotments and any other places where rich soils have been created. The leaves and stems are covered in hairs, some of which break at the tips when you brush against them, releasing several chemical compounds that cause the painful stinging sensation. These much-maligned plants do, however, have beneficial qualities for the gardener. They attract ladybirds which will devour your aphids, and their leaves can be mulched down to make an effective liquid fertilizer. You can even make a delicious healthy soup from the young tips (see Nettle soup recipe, p. 138), so it is worth allowing some to grow while not letting them go rampant.

MAY
Week 4

LETTUCES, DAISIES AND ARTICHOKES

Curiously enough, lettuces, daisies and artichokes are all part of the same family – the Asteraceae. This is one of the largest plant families – it includes weeds (dandelions and thistles), flowers (asters, daisies, chrysanthemums and sunflowers) and several edible plants (cardoon, chicory, endives, lettuce and artichokes). It takes its name from the Greek *aster* for star, based on the characteristic star-shaped flower that is in evidence in late May on all these plants.

Tie in outdoor tomatoes and pinch out. Protect them from any downpours with a plastic covering. In an allotment, let the borders go a bit wild with dandelions, daisies and nettles for the creatures that live in these spaces, but keep on top of areas around sheds and water butts to avoid getting stung by nettles. Weed areas around your vegetables, especially around globe artichokes.

JUNE INTRODUCTION

As the summer solstice approaches, you have plenty of daylight in which to work on the vegetable plot. With fears of frost gone, and the promise of plenty of sunshine, you can plant out your runner beans, broccoli, Brussels sprouts and summer cabbage. Spring onions, shallots, young turnips, summer spinach and cauliflower should be available to harvest, as well as early peas and potatoes.

Your main jobs this month will be weeding and watering. Sprinkling small amounts of water on the surface is not enough – make sure you give everything a good soaking so that the water reaches the roots. Keep the hoe busy little and often to help improve the capillary action of the soil and allow any rainwater to soak in. Now is also the time to put netting over your fruit bushes to stop birds stealing the crops.

CROPS TO SOW

Beetroot	Marrows
Carrots	Peas
Calabrese	Radish
Chicory	Runner beans
Courgettes	Spring onions
Cucumbers	Squash
Endive	Swedes
French beans	Sweetcorn
Lettuce	Turnips
Kohlrabi	

CUCKOO SPIT

This is nothing to do with the cuckoo at all. The frothy spit that appears on grasses and plants in June is the way the common frog-hopper disguises its tiny green larvae.

JUNE
Week 1

There are still many crops you can sow this month. If the weather is dry, as it should be in June, it is worth soaking your seed drill before sowing and then you can just water with a fine spray afterwards.

Dwarf and climbing French beans are especially popular and can be sown direct at this time of year. These are easy plants to grow and great to eat fresh from the earth. A combination of sunshine and watering will provide you with vigorous growth in a matter of days.

BIODEGRADABLE PEST SPRAY

Boil two crushed garlic cloves in 600ml (1 pt) water; mix in 1 tbsp of biodegradable washing up liquid. Spray this mixture on your plants to deter pests.

BIRDS IN THE GARDEN

Many birds that eat insects also eat fruit, so growing some fruit bushes encourages the birds to come along and clear up the insects. A thrush, for example, eats thousands of insects every summer and is partial to elderberry trees, while blue tits love to eat the insects on apple trees and are especially effective with aphids. You do need to protect the fruit with nets, however, or most of your crop will be gone before you have a chance to pick it. Take the nets off the crops at the end of the season.

JUNE
Week 2

Remove yellowing leaves from outdoor tomatoes and hoe over open soil and seedbeds to keep them ready for sowing and planting. Hoe through Brussels sprouts and lettuces. Give every young fruit tree a bucket of water if conditions are dry. Tie in and pinch out tomatoes and tie in runner beans where needed.

PLANTING OUT LEEKS

Lift young leeks from your nursery beds and keep them in a bucket of water until ready to plant out. Use a dibber to make planting holes 15 cm (6 in) deep and 15 cm (6 in) apart. Place one leek in each hole. Puddle-in by filling each hole with water and cover with soil. Allow the soil level to settle over the next few days.

BLACK FLY

Black fly can devastate crops at this time of year. Affected areas can be sprayed with a weak solution of washing up liquid and garlic-infused water through a hand-held mini-spray.

JUNE
Week 3

Hoe among sweetcorn and dill planted as companions. Water red cabbages. This is the last chance to plant out your Brussels sprouts. Water all your crops generously – beans and peas and globe artichokes are especially thirsty. Check all your crops and remove or destroy aphid and black fly eggs as well as beetles. Start harvesting early potatoes.

WEEDING COMPANIONS

Weeding usually brings blackbirds out, darting around the vegetable plot scouting for worms.

WEEDING

June is as good a time as any to get down and dirty with some serious weeding.

Ground elder is an invasive and persistent plant found in most allotments and in many gardens. It was introduced to England in the Middle Ages as it has wide-ranging medicinal virtues and provides relief from swollen joints, rheumatism and gout. Clearing it can be a real undertaking, though, and even when done with great care the plant is apt to return.

However, weeding does not have to be a tedious chore – it can be satisfying and meditative.

JUNE
Week 4

Tend and tie in tomatoes; if any of the plants have developed more than six or seven trusses, pinch out surplus ones so that the plant puts all its energy into producing fruit. Check for asparagus beetles. Tie up and stake runner beans. Hand weed and hoe around all plants and water regularly. Sprinkle a topdressing of wood ash and hoe on to the soil. Summer prune apple spurs. Keep control over aphids and blackfly.

SACRIFICIAL COMPANIONS

Rather than destroying butterfly caterpillars, relocate them to 'sacrificial' companion plants such as nasturtiums where they won't eat your food.

DEADLY BUTTERFLIES

Butterflies are in abundance this month. Everyone loves butterflies – they are beautiful. However, they leave behind lethal little calling cards on the underside of brassica leaves. Keep an eye out for their yellow and white eggs which rapidly hatch into a legion of crop-destroying caterpillars. Wipe the eggs off with damp kitchen paper before it is too late.

JULY INTRODUCTION

July is probably the driest month of the year and much of your time will be taken up with watering. If you were not able to get an allotment plot close to the water supply and you are having to carry heavy watering cans a long distance, you can make matters easier by spreading a thick layer of mulch around your plants to help prevent too much water loss from the soil during this time of year. Unfortunately, as well as aiding water retention this will also encourage slugs, so you will need to remain vigilant in your efforts to destroy them.

JOBS TO DO

Weed regularly so that it does not turn into a daunting task – weeds grow fast at this time of year. Plant out the remainder of your young leeks. Keep your tomato shoots in check and don't forget to feed the plants. Stay on top of pests by spraying them. Pinch out your broad beans and keep an eye out for caterpillars on your brassicas.

CROPS TO SOW

Even though it is well into the growing season there are still a few crops to sow in July:

Beetroot

Calabrese

Carrots

Chicory

Cabbage

Endives

French Beans

Kohlrabi

Lettuce

Radish

Spring onions

Turnips

JULY
Week 1

Liquid feed tomatoes to encourage the production of large, good-quality tomatoes. Water in young leeks. Harvest garlic and shallots and lay them out to dry in a sunny spot. Hand-weed and keep the hoe busy even if you can't see the weeds to aerate the dry soil. Control aphids and beetles by hand picking and spraying. This is a peak season for caterpillars, so remember to check the undersides of leaves for their presence.

CROPS TO HARVEST

Your crops should now be in abundance and you should have a plentiful supply of:

Beetroot	Onions
Broad beans	Peas
Cabbage	Peppers
Calabrese	Potatoes
Carrots	(early)
Cauliflower	Radish
Courgettes	Runner
Cucumbers	beans
French beans	Shallots
Garlic	Spinach
Kale	Spring onions
Kohlrabi	Tomatoes
Lettuce	Turnips

JULY
Week 2

Water all crops thoroughly if the weather remains dry. Harvest soft fruit such as gooseberries. Cut off Jerusalem artichoke tops to improve your harvest in the winter. Harvest spring onions. Hand-weed the vegetable plot and erect protective wire fences to try to keep out foxes and, in rural areas, badgers too. Check constantly for pests. Get up early and make the most of the long days. At this time of year birdsong will be starting to decrease as the breeding season comes to an end, so if you are in the garden or allotment early in the morning, spend a few minutes of downtime with a flask of tea just enjoying the sound of the birds singing.

PLANTING KOHLRABI

It is still not too late to plant kohlrabi, also known as turnip-rooted cabbage. Sow seeds thinly into drills 1.5 cm (¾ in) deep and 30 cm (12 in) apart. As the seedlings grow, gradually thin out the weakest specimens to allow 15 cm (6 in) between plants. They will be ready to harvest when the stem base reaches golfball size. Discard the leaves and shoots.

COOKING KOHLRABI

Steam, sauté or eat raw, grated in a salad – delicious!

JULY
Week 3

Water leeks and keep strawberries soaked. Give Brussels sprouts a good drenching, too. Gather up the dried bunches of garlic and shallots to hang in an airy place. Courgettes should be delivering their fruit. As with runner beans, the more you pick the more they deliver. Beetroots also crop prolifically in high summer.

SLICED COURGETTE SNACK

Use a potato peeler to slice courgettes into long, thin ribbons. Flash fry in some olive oil. Season with salt and pepper for a delicious all-day snack.

STEAMY BEETROOT!

Beetroot has been a popular European vegetable since the 1700s. Sweeter than many other vegetables, beetroot is full of naturally occurring sugars. The consumption of these sugars relaxes the human metabolism and provides an extraordinary sense of wellbeing with the accompaniment of very interesting aphrodisiac side-effects in some people.

JULY
Week 4

Water carrots, tomatoes and strawberries. Remove yellow leaves from the tomatoes. Drench the roots of chard and leaf beet. Use a cut-off plastic bottle sunk into the ground to water roots directly and so avoid too much unnecessary water usage (see page 19). Keep on hoeing and enjoy the long evenings.

FENNEL
Use the feathery green leaves to flavour soups. Slice the liquorice-tasting bulbs into salads.

GLOBE ARTICHOKES – THE EDIBLE THISTLE

Globe artichokes are a member of the thistle family. The flower bud is eaten before it opens, at which point it is no longer good to eat. To prepare for cooking, remove and discard the tough outer leaves and the top quarter of the artichoke. Trim the tips of the leaves with scissors. The inedible hairy 'choke' that is enclosed by the leaves needs to be pulled away, which can be done before or after boiling for 30–40 minutes in salted water acidulated with a little lemon juice.

AUGUST INTRODUCTION

August is usually another month of constant watering. Your harvest should be doing well, providing more produce than you know what to do with. Fresh vegetables that you cannot eat or give away can be stored over the winter.

STORING POTATOES

If you wish to store your early potatoes, rinse them off as soon as they come out of the ground and leave them in the sun to dry so that the skins harden. Sort the potatoes and keep the good ones for overwintering in a sack in a cool dark place. Damaged potatoes should be used straightaway. Do not store them as they may rot and then spread rot to the other stored potatoes. Check your sacks of potatoes on a regular basis for any signs of rot setting in.

CROPS TO SOW

There are still some crops you can sow in August:

Cabbage

Endives

Kohlrabi

Lettuce (winter variety)

Radish

Spinach

Turnips

AUGUST
Week 1

If your runner beans have reached the top of their supports, they will benefit from the growing tips being pinched out so that a bushy growth will develop. Keep side shoots on your tomato plants in check, and pinch out the growing tip if they have reached sufficient height in order to encourage the production of large tomatoes. As usual, stay on top of the hoeing and weeding.

AUGUST HARVEST

Your crops should now be plentiful and you should have an abundant supply of:

Aubergines	Onions
Beetroot	Peas
Broad beans	Peppers
Cabbage	Potatoes
Calabrese	(early)
Carrots	Rhubarb
Cauliflower	Runner
Celery	beans
Chicory	Radish
Courgettes	Shallots
Cucumbers	Spinach
French beans	Spring onions
Garlic	Squash
Kale	Sweetcorn
Kohlrabi	Tomatoes
Lettuce	Turnips

AUGUST
Week 2

HORSE MANURE

Working horses are rare these days, but horse-riding is a popular sport and it should not be hard to obtain horse manure from a livery stable or riding school. It is one of the best fertilizers to use, containing all the necessary nutrients for a healthy allotment. It must be well-rotted before applying. If you lack storage space to keep it while it rots down, it is usually possible to buy horse manure from a garden centre and this will be ready for use.

Control pests by spraying your plants regularly with a soap and garlic water mixture (see page 53). Turn over your compost heap to let air in, encouraging bacteria to break down the compost. If your compost becomes too dry, hose it down with some water. In the summer, compost should take only 12 weeks or so to make.

AUGUST
Week 3

Check Brussels sprouts for caterpillars and transfer any you find to nasturtiums. Tidy up overgrown vegetation and weeds from the edge of your plot and around your compost heaps. Keep on watering all container crops and beans. Hoe among the vegetable rows to keep them clear of weeds. Continue to harvest your onions.

HARVESTING AND STORING ONIONS

Onions are ripe and ready to harvest when the bulbs lift out easily. Soft bulbs are no good and should be discarded on the compost heap. Onions with brown necks should be eaten first. All the others can be tied together in bunches and hung in a sheltered, frost-free place until you want to eat them. They should store well into late spring.

COMPANION PLANTING

Growing different plants together can prove beneficial. Onions are suitable companions for broccoli, cabbage, lettuce, strawberry and tomato. (See pages 24–25.)

AUGUST
Week 4

Start getting the shallots in store. Harvest the last of your early potatoes; the maincrop will soon be ready for digging too. Keep removing caterpillars from your crops. Wild flowers on an allotment plot can be pleasing to the eye, and poppies are very much at home among vegetables. Letting some grow can help to create a balanced environment and attract beneficial insects such as bees.

POTATO HISTORY

Potatoes have been in cultivation for at least 7,000 years but they did not arrive in Europe until the 16th century, when the Spanish conquistadors brought them back from South America. It was Sir Francis Drake who introduced them to England in 1586. Europeans soon found potatoes easier to cultivate than any other crop, only requiring a shovel to harvest them. The Irish working class lived largely on potatoes but when in the 1840s a major potato blight reached Ireland their staple food disappeared. Ultimately the Irish Potato Famine led to almost a million Irish deaths and mass migration to Britain, America and Australia.

SEPTEMBER INTRODUCTION

September provides vegetable gardeners with many perfect warm sunny days for weeding. A Dutch hoe is the perfect tool for this job. Work slowly and carefully, sliding the blade back and forth through the surface without digging too deep. The weeds will be sliced off from their roots. Hoeing also aerates the soil and gives rain a chance to penetrate below the surface.

LEAF MOULD

If you have deciduous trees nearby you are in luck – the fallen autumn leaves are of great value in the vegetable plot, enhancing soil structure, retaining moisture and encouraging soil life. Collected leaves can be piled up and left to decompose. The rich, dark result is known as leaf mould and can be applied to the soil as a mulch which is easy to handle and free.

ATTRACTING WILDLIFE

Leave a pile of leaf mould in the shade to attract frogs and hedgehogs to your plot – they will eat a lot of slugs.

SEPTEMBER
Week 1

COMPOST

As you harvest your crops you will be pulling up a lot of vegetation that can go on the compost heap. Most vegetation is suitable, though it is best to avoid tomatoes, which can spread disease. Grass clippings block the passage of air and can turn into a slimy mess, so make alternate layers no more than 15 cm (6 in) thick with 'brown' compost such as dead leaves and woodchips that allow plenty of aeration.

By September your hard work earlier in the year will be paying off and you should now have plenty of crops to choose from. If you have planted a wide range of crops you could now be harvesting aubergines, beetroot, broad beans, cabbage, calabrese, carrots, cauliflower, celery, chicory, courgettes, cucumbers, endives, French beans, globe artichokes, kale, kohlrabi, lettuce, marrows, onions, peas, peppers, potatoes, pumpkins, radish, runner beans, shallots, spinach, spring onions, sweet potatoes, sweetcorn, tomatoes and turnips.

SLUGS AND SNAILS
Withered plant leaves on the ground provide hiding places for slugs and snails. Remove the leaves to a separate leaf pile to make leaf mould.

SEPTEMBER
Week 2

PLANTING WINTER ONIONS

Winter onions, sometimes called autumn or Japanese onions, are tough enough to stay out in the harsher winter months, swelling up in spring and ripening for an early harvest in June and July. Set the bulbs gently into well-prepared soil 15 cm (6 in) apart, leaving the neck above ground level. They grow large and succulent and you will need to eat them at once as they do not store well.

Your peas, broad beans, runner beans and French beans will still be producing. Once pumpkins are a deep orange colour with a firm rind, cut off the stalks and leave the pumpkins in a warm place to cure for 1–2 weeks. While there is not much to sow in September, you are still able to put in winter onions and salad plants.

SEPTEMBER
Week 3

Although your parsnips are probably a good size they may benefit from staying in the ground longer as they taste sweeter after some frost. Keep digging maincrop potatoes. Keep the hoe busy with weed removal.

WHAT'S THE DIFFERENCE?

Frogs are small, slim, agile and smooth-skinned. Toads are fat, slow and warty. Both of them love slugs.

FROGS AND TOADS

Frogs and toads eat slugs and snails, so if you can encourage their presence in the garden or allotment they can be very useful. However, they do need water to survive, especially in summer. A small pool is ideal as they will then spawn future generations on your plot. Make the pool with gently sloping sides for easy access and surround it with vegetation to provide shelter from the birds that are their main predator.

Frogs and toads spend little time in a pond outside the breeding season so it is vital to have somewhere they can hide and hibernate close by, such as an old log or overturned pot.

SEPTEMBER
Week 4

Carry on feeding your tomatoes, peppers and cucumbers for as long as they continue to grow. Tidy up summer-fruiting raspberry bushes, cutting off any canes that have fruited. Paint any wooden structures such as sheds or cold frames with preservative ready for the winter.

SLOW WORMS

Slow worms eat slugs. Putting carpet, black plastic or corrugated iron on the ground attracts them to the warmth beneath.

HEDGEHOGS

As hedgehogs eat slugs and cutworms, they are more wildlife to welcome. In winter they hibernate in piles of leaves and other vegetation, so if you build a bonfire check that no hedgehogs have taken up residence before you set it alight. Hedgehogs not only have sharp spines but an abundance of fleas; you will not need to handle them, though, as they will depart when they are disturbed.

OCTOBER INTRODUCTION

As most of your crops come to an end you will be clearing your soil beds. Instead of leaving them bare, sow some green manure – plants grown to enrich the soil. In winter they also protect the soil structure from damage by heavy rain and keep weeds down by competing for light and nutrients. Green manures that can be sown early in October include Hungarian grazing rye, Italian rye grass and winter field beans. Cut them down in spring and dig them into the soil once they have wilted a little.

COMFREY

One of the most effective green manures is comfrey, which is grown in a permanent bed and cut several times a year. The wilted leaves can be used as a mulch or turned into a liquid fertilizer. This is done by putting comfrey leaves into a barrel and adding water – one part comfrey to three parts water. After 3–5 weeks you will have an evil-smelling but very nutritious fertilizer to pour onto the soil.

CROPS TO HARVEST

Brussels sprouts, carrots, celeriac, leeks, potatoes, radish, squash, salsify, spring onions, swedes, turnips.

OCTOBER
Week 1

Check your brassicas and remove any yellow leaves as they will encourage slugs. Tidy up all the soft fruit bushes, cutting off the tips and removing any dead leaves and rotten berries.

It is time to take down your French beans and the structures that have been supporting them. Simply snip off the plants at ground level and pull up the canes. Cut the twine and bundle the canes together for safekeeping until next year. The tangle of stems and leaves can be pitchforked on top of the compost heap. Leave the roots in the ground, as they will enrich the soil with nitrogen.

FRENCH BEANS

When Christopher Columbus returned from his second voyage to the New World in 1493, French beans were among the other vegetables he brought with him that were new to Europe. They were introduced to Britain by the Huguenots – French Protestants fleeing from Louis XVI. Smaller than runner beans, they grow in the same vigorous clinging manner and are often referred to as green beans or string beans. French beans are full of dietary fibre that can help to lower cholesterol and are traditionally believed also to be beneficial to diabetics as they help to stimulate insulin levels.

OCTOBER
Week 2

Harvest your squashes and dig up and store your maincrop potatoes. Cut down outdoor tomatoes, burning the stems and leaves to prevent any winter disease. Remove dead rhubarb leaves and mulch your plants (see panel, left). Hoe weeds among winter onions and plant garlic.

MULCHING RHUBARB

Look after your rhubarb at this time of year and you will reap the benefits when you pick the first delicious pink stems in April and May next year. Now is the time to remove any decomposed leaves and stems, adding them to the compost heap. Apply a thick mulch of manure on top of the plants. As the plants lie dormant over the winter, the roots will be able to feed on the nutrients as they filter down into the soil.

GREEN TOMATOES

Large unripened tomatoes can be further ripened indoors or turned into delicious chutney.

OCTOBER
Week 3

Scarecrows are a traditionally pleasing sight, though it is not certain how effective they are at deterring birds. Pigeons can be a particular nuisance, pecking foliage and fouling crops with their droppings. Keep any bird-scaring devices in good working order to make your plot inhospitable to troublesome birds like pigeons all year round.

FROG CONSERVATION

Frogs are normally tucked up in their hideouts for winter by now, but mild days can confuse them and they can sometimes be seen out and about scouting for food. Take care to leave buckets and other steep-sided receptacles upside down, as frogs will sometimes leap in and are then unable to get out again. Trapped by the steep edges, they may drown in buckets of rainwater. If there are any vessels that cannot be overturned, leave propped-up sticks in them to provide an escape route.

OCTOBER
Week 4

A PEEK AT LEEKS

Leeks are a member of the *Allium* genus, related to garlic and onions, but they have a much subtler flavour. Leeks are cultivated widely across northern Europe and Asia. They thrive in cooler climates and tolerate frost, making them a popular winter vegetable. They have been cultivated since ancient times and legend has it that the Welsh adopted the leek as a national emblem after Saint David ordered his troops to wear them in their helmets to distinguish themselves from their Saxon foes during a battle that took place in a field of leeks.

Have a big bonfire to get rid of all rubbish which cannot be composted. Remove yellow leaves from your Brussels sprouts. Harvest your leeks, which will have a wonderful smell – eating them the same day will remind you just how much better your own home-grown food tastes.

COCK-A-LEEKIE

Cock-a-leekie soup is the delicious well-known Scottish winter soup made from chicken and leeks.

NOVEMBER INTRODUCTION

November usually means the frosts have started and it is time to harvest your winter cabbages and cauliflowers. Brussels sprouts should be starting to produce their main crop. You may still have crops of celery and celeriac as well as cabbages, carrots, jerusalem artichokes and the winter staples of turnips, parsnips and swedes. You can still plant garlic and sow hardy broad beans.

STORING APPLES

Now is a good time to be thinking about storing apples, since most people love eating them all year round. The British have grown many varieties of apples since Roman times. Each has its own special quality and distinct taste for eating, cooking and drinking. You can store apples over the winter by wrapping them individually in greaseproof paper. Bruised fruit does not keep well, so store only perfect specimens. Place the wrapped apples together in a ventilated cardboard box, handling them carefully to avoid bruising them, and store in a cool, frost-free place.

NOVEMBER
Week 1

PARSNIP SNIPPINGS

November usually sees the first frost of the year and the start of the parsnip season. Starches in the plant are turned into sugars by low temperatures, resulting in a sweet-tasting late harvest. Parsnips have been in cultivation for at least 2,000 years. For centuries in Europe they were a staple food, used to sweeten cakes and jams. Their popularity declined after sugar became more widely available, but their soft, fragrant, slightly sweet flesh still adds a warm and comforting element to winter dishes.

Take advantage of any sunny days to lift the last of the carrots and store them carefully in boxes filled with almost dry sand. Store in a cool basement or garage as close to 0°C (32°F) as possible. This should keep your carrots fresh for as long as six months if the right temperature is maintained.

Give your greenhouse a good clean. Wash it down with detergent and make sure there are no pests lurking in the frame.

ROAST PARSNIPS

Whole roast parsnips are delicious accompanied by a lemon and coriander cream dip or drizzled with honey.

NOVEMBER
Week 2

Keep cabbages and Brussels sprouts free of old foliage that might attract slugs and snails. Cut down nettles from around the compost heap. Turn over the soil in beds that have been left vacant by harvesting and dig in a mulch to improve it.

DIGGING TIPS

Digging is a strenuous activity but it can be satisfying. It is easy to get carried away and dig for too long with the result that you get a backache that may take a while to ease. With a sensible approach you can enjoy this physical exercise without doing yourself any harm, so take a break every 20 minutes and do some bending and stretching. Always scrape mud off the tools after a session – clean equipment is much nicer to use than tools caked with mud before you have even begun.

NOVEMBER
Week 3

Cut down and clear vegetation among fruit trees and keep their bases weed-free. Transplant wild flowers such as foxgloves out of the vegetable patch to some spare ground nearby so that they will still be there to attract pollinating insects next spring. Burn other accumulated garden debris.

BURNING RUBBISH

Start the fire next to the debris to be burnt rather than under it. Given the cold November nights, a few frogs, toads and hedgehogs may have chosen your pile of rubbish as a shelter, so make sure you do not accidentally incinerate them. Light some crumpled newspaper to get the fire started and then fork on the debris, taking care not to scoop up any wildlife.

On an allotment, check the rules about fires. Garden incinerators are readily available from DIY stores and are usually made of galvanized steel. They come complete with a chimney lid and ready-made ventilation holes to ensure efficient combustion.

NOVEMBER
Week 4

Check the vegetables and fruit you have in store to make sure that any produce that looks as if it is going to rot is removed before it spreads rot among its neighbours. If you are using your greenhouse during winter it will need insulating. Bubble wrap is ideal, but do not forget to leave a small amount of ventilation in order to avoid mould forming.

PLANTING GARLIC

Break up the garlic bulbs and plant the cloves upright with the pointed end just below the surface, about 15 cm (6 in) apart. Cold spells stimulate growth and the development of strong roots, and the shoots should be well developed by the New Year. Harvest in summer when the foliage turns brown, lifting the bulbs carefully to avoid damage. Use some immediately and hang the rest in a sheltered place to dry out.

THE HEALTHY CLOVE

Eating garlic regularly is believed to ward off heart disease, cancer, colds and even influenza.

DECEMBER INTRODUCTION

Good soil is one of the gardener's most valuable assets; care and attention spent at this time of year will reap rewards in the spring and summer as successive healthy crops are harvested. Not only must nutrition be put back into the ground by regular batches of organic manure, but the surface must also be tended to keep it weed-free and aerated. Humus-rich soil will stand up much better to hot summer weather than poor, thin soil.

TIME TO RELAX

Use December to relax, knock the mud off your wellies and dream about what you want to grow in your vegetable plot next year – give yourself a well-earned rest.

MILLIPEDES AND CENTIPEDES

There are more than 10,000 known species of millipede worldwide and probably more to be discovered. One African species grows to more than 30 cm (12 in), though our British species rarely exceed 4 cm (1½ in). They breed in spring and summer and lay up to 100 eggs which hatch out in 2–3 weeks. As they grow the number of millipede body segments increases up to around 50, each with two pairs of legs. They hibernate in winter but while active are a garden pest, attacking the roots of seedlings, root vegetables, bulbs and tubers. Centipedes have only one set of legs per segment, are reddish and are faster-moving than millipedes. They feed on slugs and are therefore a very welcome resident in the vegetable plot.

DECEMBER
Weeks 1 & 2

Winter has truly set in, and the short days mean that there is not so much time in which to work on your plot. However, you can continue to harvest leeks, parsnips, salsify and scorzonera through the winter. Brussels sprouts are still in the soil too, ready to be picked for Christmas dinner.

VEGETABLE STORE

Keep a careful eye on the store of vegetables that you have accumulated. Rotting potatoes smell really bad, which is a warning sign to be alert to. Remove them gently and dispose of them.

Potatoes kept in trays in the dark are easier to inspect than those in sacks, which have to be emptied to check the contents.

ONIONS IN STORE

Immediately use any onions that are starting to sprout and watch out for any with foul-smelling slime oozing from the roots as this will contaminate the others.

Keep Brussels sprouts plants tidy by removing the oldest foliage. Hand-weed the plot and check over all areas for slugs and snails. Clean up all the dirty used pots with a weak mix of water and washing up liquid.

DECEMBER
Weeks 3 & 4

Weed turnips and remove decaying foliage to the compost heap. Check for slugs and snails and burn any rubbish they can hide beneath. Select the best of your winter harvest to give to friends and family. Enjoy sunny days by pottering around thinking about next year's planting.

GROWING SHALLOTS

Shallots are traditionally planted on the shortest day of the year. Grow them in a sunny bed, raked level, at 15 cm (6 in) intervals in rows 30 cm (12 in) apart. Press each one into the soil gently, with the tip just above soil level. They can be pulled in early to late summer in dry sunny weather. When they are ripe, the multiple bulbs break apart freely.

NATURAL SOIL MANAGEMENT

The water in soil expands as it solidifies in response to freezing night-time temperatures then contracts when it thaws during the day. This freezing and thawing helps air and moisture to permeate the ground and creates a fine springtime soil without any assistance. A light turning over of the soil with a hoe or rake on a chilly day helps to expose any undesirable pests.

Prepare and plant shallots (see panel, left) and tend kale by stripping away yellow and brown leaves for compost. You can also begin to harvest it now, with the expectation that you can carry on cutting it until early spring.

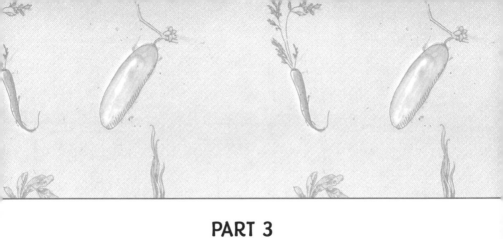

PART 3

A–Z
WHAT TO PLANT
WHERE AND WHEN

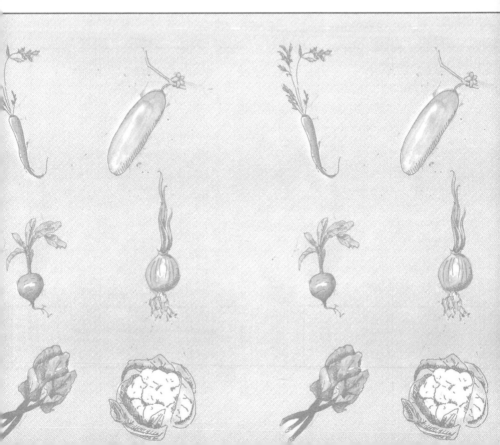

AUBERGINES

Aubergines are available in several varieties with slightly different shapes and colours. You should grow them under protection in all but the mildest areas; even in mild areas, aubergines are most reliable when grown in a greenhouse or polytunnel. If you are planting outdoors, choose the sunniest, most sheltered spot available. Warm the soil by covering it with black plastic before planting. Set out the plants in late spring or early summer and cover with fleece or cloches until established. Pinch out the tops when the plants reach 38 cm (15 in) tall and feed with tomato fertilizer throughout the growing season. In a greenhouse or polytunnel, keep well watered at all times, spraying them frequently to maintain a humid atmosphere.

CULTIVATION

Sowing

Sow seeds indoors in warmth (18°C/65°F) in March or in a cold greenhouse in April. Scatter thinly on the surface of the compost and cover with a light layer of vermiculite.

Transplanting

When the seedlings are about 5 cm (2 in) high, prick out into 7.5 cm (3 in) pots. Harden off by putting outside on warm days; when flowers appear, plant outside, spaced about 45 cm (18 in) apart.

Soil and site

Fertile, well-drained soil in a sheltered position.

Harvesting

From late summer to mid-autumn.

Expert tip

Dwarf aubergines can be grown in containers in a sunny spot.

BEANS: BROAD AND FRENCH

CULTIVATION

Sowing

Broad beans can be sown in autumn if your plot is sheltered and has free-draining soil; otherwise sow outside from March to May, 3 cm (1½ in) deep and 23 cm (9 in) apart. Sow French beans outside from late spring to early summer at the same depth and distance.

Soil and site

Fertile, moisture-retentive but not waterlogged soil in a warm, sheltered spot. They crop best on neutral to slightly acid soils.

Harvesting

From early summer to early autumn.

Expert tip

Do not grow broad beans in the same site two years running as this may cause a build-up of pea cyst eelworm in the soil.

Broad and French beans are favourite crops for gardeners. They are easy to grow and ideal for those cultivating a vegetable plot for the first time. Climbing French beans can be grown up poles like runner beans (see page 88), or you can opt for the compact bush type, which will also grow in bags or containers.

You can harvest French beans young and eat them whole, or allow them to mature and then dry the beans for winter use as haricot beans.

Beans usually have few problems as long as you plant them in healthy soil and care for them properly. However, they are prone to blackfly clustered in the growing tips. Pinch out the tips and spray with a water and washing-up liquid mix. Plant marigolds to attract ladybirds, which will eat the blackfly.

BEANS, RUNNER

Runner beans are by far the most popular type of climbing bean. A vegetable plot at the height of the growing season would seem incomplete without a wigwam of these scarlet-flowered plants making an eye-catching feature. In fact, it was the flowers they were originally cultivated for until the beans were found to be edible in the 18th century. You can add to the display they make in your plot by combining them with other climbing plants such as clematis.

When planting runner beans, take into consideration that with their height and dense foliage they can cast deep shade over quite a wide area; where you site them will be critical if you have a small plot. Sow some extra seeds at the end of rows so that you have replacements if some in the row fail to germinate.

CULTIVATION

Sowing

Sow outdoors at a depth of 5 cm (2 in) in late spring to early summer, spacing 15 cm (6 in) apart around a wigwam or at the base of poles or netting. Alternatively, sow in pots under glass in mid-spring and transplant in late spring to early summer when all danger of frost is over.

Soil and site

Runner beans like a rich, moist soil, so dig in plenty of manure or compost a few months ahead of planting. They prefer full sun but will tolerate some shade in a sheltered spot. Keep well watered.

Harvesting

From summer until early autumn; it is essential to pick the pods before the beans swell so that the plants will continue to crop.

BEETROOT

Beetroot is very easy to grow, thriving under most conditions and afflicted by few pests. It is a very versatile crop, providing food from both the young leaves for salad and the roots for boiling or roasting. You can also grate raw beetroot into salads.

For March-sown crops, use bolt-resistant varieties. Sow the main crop from April onwards in small successive sowings every three weeks until midsummer for a continuous harvest through until autumn. To store, lift the roots in October. Twist off the leaves, leaving about 5 cm (2 in) stalks, and pack the roots between layers of dry peat in a box. Place in a shed, where they will keep until March.

Remember that like other root vegetables, beetroot should not be planted in recently manured soil as this can cause misshapen roots.

CULTIVATION

Sowing

Sow seeds 2.5 cm (1 in) deep in rows 30 cm (12 in) apart. Seed is usually in clusters, so once seedlings are about 2.5 cm (1 in) high thin them to 15 cm (6 in) apart. In March, sow under cloches; the main sowing season is late April to July.

Soil and site

Beetroot is not fussy, but the ideal soil is light and fertile. Choose a sunny site and prepare the soil in winter, adding compost if it is low in humus. Add lime to acid soils. Once the plants are growing, keep the soil well watered to avoid woody, split roots.

Harvesting

From July to October. When the roots are golf-ball size, pull up alternate plants for cooking. Leave the rest to mature and pull up as needed.

BROCCOLI

Broccoli and calabrese are both members of the brassica family. It is usually the green-headed calabrese that is sold in supermarkets as broccoli, rather than the true purple- or white-headed sprouting broccoli. If you grow calabrese, the variety 'Romanesco' is strikingly pretty and is not often found in the supermarkets, so it is a good choice.

Both types are easy to grow, but do not plant them on a site that has been used for brassicas in the past two years as this will increase the chances of disease. As broccoli is an over-wintering crop, give it a sheltered spot. It is a cut-and-come again vegetable, each plant cropping for about six weeks.

CULTIVATION

Sowing

Sow broccoli outdoors in seed drills in mid-spring. Sow calabrese in situ from early spring to midsummer as it does not transplant well. Sow seed of both 1 cm (½ in) deep, calabrese 2–3 seeds 15 cm (6 in) apart for later thinning.

Transplanting

From June to July, transplant broccoli into rows 60 cm (24 in) apart, spacing the plants at a distance of about 45 cm (18 in).

Soil and site

Moisture-retentive but well-drained, rich soil in sun.

Harvesting

Cut calabrese from early summer to late autumn; cut broccoli the following spring.

BRUSSELS SPROUTS

CULTIVATION

Sowing

Sow in seed drills at a depth of 1 cm (½ in), early varieties in March and late varieties in April. Thin seedlings to about 7.5 cm (3 in) apart.

Transplanting

Plant out early varieties in early May, late varieties in June. Set plants at least 60 cm (24 in) apart.

Soil and site

Enrich the soil with compost or manure in autumn or winter, adding lime if it is acid. A sheltered site is needed.

Harvesting

From September to February, cut the sprouts from the base of the stems upwards, using a sharp knife.

Another member of the brassica family, Brussels sprouts like cold frosty winters, producing their main crop from late October through to February. Transplant seedlings when they are about 15 cm (6 in) high, watering them the day before. Lift carefully with plenty of soil around the rootballs then firm them into the soil. Water the young plants well if the weather is dry; once they are established this is no longer necessary as long as the soil has been well-prepared, except in particularly dry conditions. Earth up the stems as the plants grow to keep them stable, especially once autumn is drawing near. Watch out for cabbage root fly, clubroot, caterpillars and slugs and snails. If pigeons attack the leaves, put netting over the crop.

CABBAGES

Cabbages are one of the easiest members of the brassica family to grow. The best known of the winter cabbages are Savoy and January King, the latter with smoother, less dense leaves; harvest as needed. Cut red and white cabbages no later than midwinter and store in a frost-free place; they will keep until March. Thin out spring cabbages in March and cook the plants you have removed as spring greens.

Clubroot manifests itself as discoloured, wilting leaves – remove affected plants and burn. Cabbage caterpillars can reduce leaves to shreds. Pigeons can also have a go at your cabbages, so cover with netting. Slugs and snails are a constant menace. To prevent cabbage root fly, put a 15 cm (6 in) diameter collar of carpet underlay or thick cardboard round the base of each plant.

CULTIVATION

Sowing

Sow spring cabbages July to August; summer cabbages March to April; winter varieties April to May. Sow in shallow drills; thin to 7.5 cm (3 in) apart.

Transplanting

When the seedlings have 5–6 leaves, plant in the final position. Set 45 cm (18 in) apart for large heads, 30 cm (12 in) for small heads.

Soil and site

Cabbages require a fertile, well-drained soil, with manure dug in several months before planting. They will not tolerate acid soil, so add lime if necessary. They need a fairly sunny position.

Harvesting

Cut when heads are firm, from summer to late winter.

CARROTS

CULTIVATION

Sowing

For early crops, sow short-rooted varieties under cloches in March or in a sheltered position in late March to April. Sow maincrop varieties in succession from mid-April to July. Sow thinly, 1 cm (½ in) deep.

Soil and site

Light, well-drained, deep soil, not recently manured, in a sunny position. Water the soil regularly but gently to prevent the roots from splitting.

Harvesting

Pull out individual carrots by hand as required from midsummer to early winter. If your soil is heavy, lift carrots before winter and store in boxes of sand.

Get the conditions right and carrots are one of the easiest vegetables to grow. Easy to store and rich in vitamin A and calcium, they can give you a year-round supply if planned correctly. Carrot fly is the main pest to look out for as the larvae will tunnel into your carrots. The first step towards avoiding it is to sow seed sparsely so that it does not need thinning – the scent of bruised foliage will attract these pests. Other ploys are planting onions in between the rows of carrots as their stronger smell will mask that of carrots; laying fleece over the crop; or, rather surprisingly, erecting a fine mesh or plastic fence about 45 cm (18 in) high all round the crop. Carrot flies are low-flying and will skirt around it.

CAULIFLOWER

Cauliflowers are very temperamental and probably the most difficult of the brassicas to grow. Conditions that are too hot, too cold or too dry can give disappointing results, but can be partially avoided by regular watering and, in a hot summer, bending large leaves over the heads of the cauliflowers to prevent scorching.

There are two types of cauliflower – summer and winter. The summer variety is the white-headed version that we are all familiar with, while the winter cauliflower is a type of broccoli with a green and purple head. Winter varieties, like their calabrese cousins, are much more tolerant and will grow in any soil.

As with other brassicas, the main problems are cabbage root fly, clubroot, caterpillars and pigeon damage.

CULTIVATION

Sowing
Sow summer varieties under glass in January and February for a June to July crop and outdoors in mid-April for harvesting in August and September; sow winter varieties in May. Sow seed thinly, 1 cm (½ in) deep. Thin seedlings to 7.5 cm (3 in) apart.

Transplanting
Move to their final growing position 6–8 weeks after sowing. Water beforehand and lift with as much soil as possible. Set 38–60 cm (15–24 in) apart and with 60–90 cm (24–36 in) between rows.

Soil and site
Provide rich, alkaline soil in a sunny and sheltered position.

Harvesting
Cut the stems below the head from June to November.

CELERIAC

Celeriac is a close relative of celery and has a similar flavour. The swollen, fat stem-base can be cooked or grated into salads. Celeriac does not tolerate heat well until it is established, so if the weather is sunny during the hardening-off period give the young plants some shade each day. Once planted out, provide plenty of water to keep the soil cool and damp. In all but the colder areas of the UK you can overwinter celeriac in the soil if you cover the base with mulch. In cold regions you should dig the crop in autumn and store in boxes of sand in a cool shed. Celeriac is ready to pick when the stem-base is 10 cm (4 in) in diameter.

CULTIVATION

Sowing

Sow indoors in early spring; the easiest way is to sow in modules, putting 2–3 seeds in each one and then thinning.

Transplanting

Before planting out in May or June, harden off the seedlings by placing them outside in the daytime only for 7–10 days. Plant out 30 cm (12 in) apart, setting the join between the leaves and the stem at soil level.

Soil and site

Fertile, well-drained soil, enriched the winter before. Best in a sunny, warm spot.

Harvesting

Lift from mid-autumn to late winter. In most areas you can leave them in the ground until required.

CELERY

There are three main types of celery: leaf, trench and self-blanching. You can grow leaf celery in containers as it is a small plant used for salad leaves. Trench celery needs a lot of attention and experience to be successful. Traditionally grown in a 30 cm (12 in) deep trench that is gradually filled in, the stems are blanched as they grow. Nowadays most trench celery is surface-grown with plastic collars tied loosely around the stems to blanch them. However, most popular with home gardeners are the self-blanching varieties, which are grown in a block rather than rows to provide shade for each other. The instructions given here are for this type.

The two main problems with celery are bolting and slugs. Avoid the former by never letting the soil dry out; control the latter by vigilance.

CULTIVATION

Sowing

In March or April, sow on the surface of compost and cover with a thin layer of vermiculite. Put in a heated propagator on a windowsill or in a greenhouse. When the first leaves have formed, transfer to 7.5 cm (3 in) pots.

Transplanting

When the seedlings are 7.5 cm (3 in) tall, harden off and plant out in a block with about 20 cm (8 in) between the plants. Push straw between the outer plants.

Soil and site

Deep fertile soil, moist at all times, in a warm and sheltered position.

Harvesting

Lift from August until the first frosts.

CHICORY

CULTIVATION

Sowing

Sow seeds of radicchio from mid-spring to midsummer and sugar loaf chicory in midsummer. Sow direct, 1 cm (½ in) deep, in rows 30 cm (12 in) apart. When the seedlings reach 2.5 cm (1 in) tall, thin to about 30 cm (12 in) apart.

Soil and site

Add manure the previous winter. Dig and rake the site thoroughly, removing stones and weeds. Chicory thrives in sunshine but tolerates shade.

Harvesting

If you plant several varieties you will be able to harvest from summer to winter.

Expert tip

If the outer leaves are mushy after a frost you can still use the heart.

There are three types of chicory: red chicory (radicchio), sugar loaf chicory (similar to lettuce) and Belgian chicory. However, it is rare for home gardeners to cultivate the last type, which is grown in the dark during the winter months in order to produce the blanched creamy-white shoots.

Chicory tolerates most soils except heavy, wet ones and is easy to grow and to harvest – you can snip the leaves as you need them or alternatively cut off whole heads. If you leave about 2.5cm (1 in) of stem it will resprout.

Chicory will suffer from cutworm and swift moth caterpillars if they are already on your plot. Like most of the food you are trying to grow, it is attractive to slugs.

CUCUMBER

Cucumbers are more tender than other members of the squash family but should not be overlooked by the domestic gardener. The ridge varieties are suitable for growing outdoors and will give you an abundance of fruit if harvested regularly. They are smaller and have a rougher skin than greenhouse cucumbers, but possess a superior flavour and are easier to grow.

Except for the bush varieties, cucumbers can be trained up supports. If you do not wish to do this, it is still a good idea to provide some sort of frame to lift them off the ground clear of soggy soil, slugs and snails.

Do not allow cucumbers to dry out, especially during the flowering and fruiting stages, as they rely on plenty of moisture for good fruit development.

CULTIVATION

Sowing

Sow direct in late spring to early summer, 1 cm (½ in) deep and 60 cm (2 ft) apart. Sow 2–3 seeds per station and remove the weaker seedlings. In cooler regions, protect with cloches.

Soil and site

Well-drained, humus-rich soil in a sunny spot protected from wind.

Harvesting

Pick before the fruit gets too large or you risk them becoming bitter. Cut them with a sharp knife rather than pulling them as this can damage the plant.

Expert tip

Mist plants lightly in hot weather to aid pollination. Once the fruits start to swell, feed with a good fertilizer.

ENDIVE

CULTIVATION

Sowing

Sow seeds 1 cm (½ in) deep in drills, the curly varieties from March to August and the broad-leaved varieties from July to September. Thin to 38 cm (15 in) apart. Continue to sow at monthly intervals for a long-lasting crop.

Soil and site

Endives do best in light, well-drained soil that has been treated with well-rotted manure. They like full sun but will tolerate partial shade.

Harvesting

From summer to winter, cut-and-come-again when the hearts are saucer-sized. Cut off the whole head, leaving about 2.5 cm (1 in) of stem, and the plant will resprout.

There are both curly and broad-leaved varieties of endive, all of which have a peppery taste. Make sure you prepare the soil well in advance of planting endive by working well-rotted manure into the soil. Feed them from time to time with a liquid fertilizer and water well in dry weather.

You can eliminate the slightly bitter taste of endive by blanching the leaves about 12 weeks after sowing. To do this you can either cover each plant with a large clay pot (blocking the drainage hole) or a bucket; or you can tie up the outer leaves with a strip of cloth or a wide rubber band. Make sure the leaves are absolutely dry to discourage disease. The heads will be blanched in three weeks during summer or five weeks in winter.

GARLIC

Do not be tempted to plant garlic from a supermarket to save buying it elsewhere – it will probably be a variety suited to a hotter climate. Instead, buy from a nursery or seed supplier. You will see that the varieties are described as 'softneck' or 'hardneck' – the former store better, but if this is not important try several varieties and plant your future crop according to the flavour you like best.

Each garlic bulb will consist of up to 20 individual cloves and these are individually planted. Gently remove the outer skin from the bulb and select only the largest and healthiest cloves. Garlic will benefit from an application of nitrogen in March and May. The only other requirement is to keep it free of weeds and make sure you keep it watered in dry conditions.

CULTIVATION

Planting

Plant in late autumn to early winter, setting the cloves in the soil pointed end upwards, 1–2 cm (½–1 in) deep so that the tip is just below the surface. Plant at a distance of 15 cm (6 in) in rows 30 cm (12 in) apart.

Soil and site

Light, fertile soil in full sun. Dig the soil well to a spade's depth before planting. Incorporate as much organic matter as possible to help with drainage as garlic will rot if it lies in water. Digging some sand into your garlic bed will improve the drainage even further.

Harvesting

Harvest when the foliage has turned yellowy-brown, in midsummer.

GLOBE ARTICHOKE

CULTIVATION

Planting

Because seed-raised plants are very variable, growing from offsets (rooted suckers) is best. Plant shallowly in April or early May, 1.2 m (4 ft) apart with 75 cm (2½ ft) between rows.

Soil and site

Fertile, light, well-drained soil in full sun; some shade is tolerated in warm areas. The previous autumn, dig in plenty of well-rotted manure.

Harvesting

In summer the following year.

Expert tip

The plants live only about 3–4 years, but you can cut your own offsets for the next planting. Scrape the soil from the top of the plant and cut away the offsets with a knife or spade, leaving a few on the parent plant.

This perennial is grown for its edible flower buds, but it is attractive in its own right and will be a pleasure to see in the vegetable plot. It is a big, bushy plant that grows to 1.5 m (5ft) tall, so make sure you do not plant a group where they will cast shade over a crop that needs full sun. Keep the plants well watered once they are established, making sure they do not dry out in hot weather, and feed regularly. Prevent the plants from flowering in their first year by pinching out all the flower buds, which will encourage side shoots to grow. In year two, minimize your harvesting to just five or six buds – cut the terminal bud, known as the king head, first, with about 2.5 cm (1 in) of stem attached. Cut down the stems in autumn and in colder areas protect crowns with straw over the winter.

HERBS

Herbs can be planted between your other crops and most will not require a lot of space. They can be grown either from cuttings or from seeds.

Cuttings are taken in summer. Snip off a piece about 7–10 cm (3–4 in) long from the side shoots of a healthy plant. Trim to just below a node (where a leaf joins the stem) and remove the leaves from the lower third of the stem. Using a dibber, make a hole in compost in a pot or seed tray and insert the cutting. Firm down, water gently and place in a warm, sunny spot.

When your cuttings have developed roots and are ready to plant out, sage, mint, thyme, chives and oregano love a sunny spot and the warmth will bring their oils to the surface of the leaves.

GUIDE TO HERBS
Perennial
Chives
Lovage
Mint
Oregano
Rosemary
Sage
Tarragon
Thyme
Annual
Basil
Borage
Chervil
Coriander
Dill
Parsley

Parsley, chervil and coriander prefer partial shade.

Herbs can be used as companion plants to attract helpful insects, deter pests and add nutrients to the soil that will benefit particular crops.

BENEFICIAL HERBS

Basil is thought to repel flies and mosquitoes and is said to improve the growth and flavour of tomatoes.

Borage is beneficial to strawberries, tomatoes and squash. It will attract bees to your vegetable plot and thus aid pollination.

Chamomile is helpful to onion, cabbage and cucumber.

Chives may prevent scab in apple trees if planted at the base. They are beneficial to many plants, including carrots, brassicas and tomatoes, and repel aphids and carrot fly. Chives soaked in water make a great spray to kill powdery mildew.

Dill is a good companion to cabbage, lettuce, corn, onions and cucumbers. It attracts bees and hoverflies and repels aphids.

Lovage is the gardener's friend as it is beneficial to most plants and makes a great tea, too.

Mint is good for aubergines, beetroot, tomatoes, peppers and potatoes and repels slugs.

Oregano is beneficial for tomatoes and peppers and repels aphids.

Parsley helps corn and tomatoes but should not be planted near onions and lettuce.

Rosemary is beneficial planted close to brassicas and beans, but do not put close to tomatoes. It repels cabbage fly.

Sage is a good companion to cabbage but not cucumbers.

Tarragon enhances the growth and flavour of most plants and its scent deters many pests.

Thyme repels cabbage white butterfly. Its scent attracts bees and is believed to stimulate the growth of nearby plants.

JERUSALEM ARTICHOKE

The Jerusalem artichoke bears no relation to the globe artichoke; it produces edible tubers which have a nutty flavour and make a famously good soup.

These plants can grow to about 3 m (10 ft), so plant them where the shade they cast will not be a problem for your other crops. As the stems are quite fragile they will need to be supported with stakes and string unless they are in a sheltered position. When the plants are about 30 cm (12 in) high, earth up a little to provide some stability.

When the foliage changes colour in autumn, cut it down and put it on the compost heap – but leave at least 7.5 cm (3 in) above the ground so that you can find your tubers. If you do not wish the plants to grow the following year, you will need to dig up every one.

CULTIVATION

Planting

Plant tubers in early to mid-spring, setting them about 12 cm (5 in) deep and 60 cm (24 in) apart.

Soil and site

Jerusalem artichokes are not fussy but will thrive best in rich, well-drained soil. Incorporate plenty of compost or well-rotted manure before planting since they will continue to grow in the same spot year after year if they are allowed to – they can become invasive.

Harvesting

In winter, dig up when required.

Expert tip

Water until they are well established, after which they will not need watering except in a particularly dry spell.

LEEKS

CULTIVATION

Sowing

For an early crop, sow indoors in mid to late winter. Outdoors, sow thinly in seed drills in early to mid-spring, 1 cm (½ in) deep.

Transplanting

When the seedlings are 20 cm (8 in) tall in early to midsummer, water the seedbed well. Using a dibber, make holes 15 cm (6 in) deep and the same distance apart. Lift the seedlings, transfer to the holes and fill the holes with water to settle them in. Do not add soil.

Soil and site

Moist, light soil in sun. Dig in compost or well-rotted manure the previous winter.

Harvesting

Depending on variety, from mid-autumn to early spring.

The leek is an extremely versatile vegetable suitable for cooler climates. This member of the onion family is very easy to grow and, provided the soil is not waterlogged, is not too fussy about the conditions.

Make sure you water the young plants well, especially in dry conditions, until they have become established. Apply a fertilizer to encourage thick stems, but after late August do not feed plants that you want to leave in the ground over winter. Avoid nitrogen-rich fertilizers as they make the plants more prone to rust. Keep weeds down by hoeing regularly.

If you want to increase the length of white stem, blanch the leeks by earthing up or tying cardboard around them. To harvest, ease them gently out of the soil with a fork to avoid damage.

LETTUCE & SALAD LEAVES

Of all the crops, lettuces and salad leaves are among the easiest to cultivate. Although lettuces are not too fussy about the soil it is essential that it is raked into a fine tilth before sowing as the seeds are so small. They will need plenty of water during summer – the ground should never become dry or they will bolt (go to seed). Loose-leaf varieties such as 'Lolla Rossa' and 'Royal Red Oakleaf' will not only add different colours and flavours on your plate, they are less likely to bolt. Corn salad (lamb's lettuce) can be grown for summer cropping, but sown in autumn it will also give you salad leaves for the winter. Other easy-to-grow salad plants that will provide a winter harvest include mizuna, mibuna, mustard and winter purslane; sow outdoors in early autumn.

CULTIVATION

Sowing

Sow lettuce at fortnightly intervals from early spring to midsummer, about 1 cm (½ in) deep in rows 15–30 cm (6–12 in) apart, depending on the size of the variety. Thin out once the first true leaves appear. Sow under glass from autumn onwards for a winter crop.

Soil and site

Light, fertile, well-drained soil in a sheltered spot, out of full midday sun.

Harvesting

Pull up lettuces such as cos and crispheads 8–14 weeks after sowing, depending on variety. Harvest as soon as the hearts are formed, as they will bolt soon afterwards. Pick loose-leaf varieties a few leaves at a time from 6 weeks after sowing.

ONIONS

No vegetable plot would be complete without a row of onions. There are a number of varieties, including the sweeter white and red ones as well as the familiar yellow-skinned type, and all are easy to grow. The easiest way to start onions off is to plant sets rather than seeds, though your choice of varieties will be more limited. Sets are immature onion bulbs that have been raised specially for planting, some being treated to make them less likely to bolt; these are the best option. You must be diligent about dealing with weeds as they will quickly take over your onion bed. Make sure you keep the young onions watered during dry spells, but stop once they are in their final stages of maturing. Plant carrots and parsnips nearby to deter onion fly.

CULTIVATION

Planting

Plant sets in early to mid spring, 10 cm (4 in) apart in rows about 25 cm (10 in) apart. Push them into the soil with the tips just above the surface. Sow seeds indoors from midwinter.

Transplanting

Harden off seed-grown onions and plant out in early spring at the same spacing as sets.

Soil and site

Fertile, well-drained, neutral to alkaline soil, well-manured the previous autumn, in a sunny position.

Harvesting

Pull up when the foliage becomes withered in summer and autumn. If not using immediately, allow them to dry in a warm place for 1–2 weeks before storing.

PARSNIPS

The main problem with growing parsnips on your vegetable plot is that they are slow to mature and can take up valuable space for almost a year. However, they are one of the few vegetables that are available through the winter and they actually become sweeter and tastier after the first frosts.

The soil is probably the most important factor as it needs to be light, deep and raked free of stones. Level the bed off to give a fine tilth before sowing parsnips. If your soil is heavy, choose short-rooted varieties.

In a dry spell, make sure that you water your parsnips regularly – if you allow them to dry out and then give them plenty of water the roots are liable to split.

Canker is the main problem with parsnips – choose resistant varieties.

CULTIVATION

Sowing

Sow seed in spring, 1 cm (½ in) deep in rows about 30 cm (12 in) apart. Thin the seedlings to 15 cm (6 in) apart. Alternatively, sow several seeds at stations at that distance and keep only the strongest seedling at each station.

Soil and site

An open, sunny site with light, deep, humus-rich soil that is stone-free and neutral to alkaline.

Harvesting

The crop will be ready from mid-autumn; leave in the ground until needed or store in a box of sand in a shed.

Expert tip

Discard any unused seeds after sowing, since parsnip seeds only germinate if they are fresh.

PEAS

CULTIVATION

Sowing
Sow early round varieties outdoors from February to March, marrowfat varieties and mangetouts from April. Maincrop varieties can be sown as late as June for a September crop. Sow seed 2.5–5 cm (1–2 in) deep in rows 60–90 cm (2–3 ft) apart and thin to about 7.5 cm (3 in) apart.

Soil and site
Fertile, moisture-retentive, neutral to alkaline soil. Do not use high-nitrogen fertilizer.

Harvesting
While pods are still young.

Expert tip
Peas extract nitrogen from the air and store it in their roots, so when you have finished cropping, leave the roots in the soil.

Peas come in early and maincrop varieties, so you can plant with a view to cropping from mid-May to mid-September. Pick regularly, since the yield will be reduced if you allow mature pods to remain on the plants. Harvest from the bottom of the plants upwards once the peas are nearly touching in the pods, with the exception of mangetouts, which are picked at about 7.5 cm (3 in) long, before the peas develop. Pick peas as near to eating as possible to enjoy them at their best.

Some varieties can grow quite tall, which means they will shade neighbouring plants. All varieties will need support with canes or netting.

Mice and birds are fond of the seeds, so cover them with netting or twigs immediately after sowing.

PEPPERS

Both sweet and chilli peppers will need to be started off indoors and unless you have a warm, sheltered area in the vegetable plot they are best grown entirely under glass. Once they reach about 30 cm (12 in) tall, pinch out the growing tip of the main shoot to increase the strength of the plant, since the fruits are quite heavy. As soon as you see the first flowers, feed each week with a liquid feed rich in potash, such as a tomato food.

If you lack space, peppers grow quite happily in large pots or grow bags, but you must remember to water and feed them regularly.

Peppers will keep for up to two weeks in a sealed container in the bottom of your refrigerator. Sweet peppers can be blanched and then frozen; hang chilli peppers up to dry.

CULTIVATION

Sowing

Sow indoors 1 cm (½ in) deep in pots or trays from late winter at 21°C (70°F). Once seedlings appear, maintain a temperature of 12–15°C (60–65°F). When they are 5 cm (2 in) high, prick out into pots.

Transplanting

When the plants flower in late spring or early summer, harden them off and plant out, about 45 cm (18 in) apart.

Soil and site

Well-drained, fertile and moisture-retentive soil, preferably acid, in a very sheltered spot.

Harvesting

From midsummer to early autumn.

Expert tip

Mist peppers in the greenhouse to discourage red spider mite and greenfly.

POTATOES

CULTIVATION

Planting

Plant first earlies in late March, 30 cm (12 in) apart and 10 cm (4 in) deep in rows 45 cm (18 in) apart; second earlies in early to mid April at 38 cm (15 in) intervals in rows 75 cm (30 in) apart; maincrop in mid to late April, spaced the same.

Soil and site

An open, sunny position and deep soil with compost or manure dug in the previous autumn. Slightly acid soil is best.

Harvesting

Eat earlies as soon as they are dug from June to August; maincrop from September onwards. To store, cut off the haulms once withered and lift the tubers 10 days later. Allow to dry for a few hours then store in a frost-free shed.

Potatoes fall into three types – first earlies, second earlies and maincrop – and if you plant some of each you will be able to harvest your own potatoes from June to October. 'Chitting' is essential for earlies and advisable for maincrops; put seed potatoes in trays indoors, with the blunt end uppermost. Place in a cool area with good light and shoots will start to appear. Do not use supermarket potatoes as they may carry virus.

After planting out, when the haulms (leaves) reach about 23 cm (9 in) high, pull soil over the stems from either side to form a ridge – called 'earthing up'. This protects the plants from late frosts and also stops the tubers from becoming green, when they are poisonous. Repeat this process regularly until the ridges are about 15 cm (6 in) high.

RADISHES

Radishes are just about the fastest and easiest vegetable to grow. There are two varieties, winter and summer, and all they require is a loose soil that has been treated with some organic matter. If you sow every two weeks or so, you will have a continuous harvest. Don't allow summer radishes to get too large, as they will become woolly-textured and hot – the size of a marble is about right.

Winter radishes, such as the daikon types, grow larger than the summer varieties but do take longer to mature. However, they will keep longer in storage.

All radishes appreciate plenty of water and it is a good idea to mulch to keep weeds down to a minimum. Radishes will benefit from a fertilizer high in potassium and phosphorus.

CULTIVATION

Sowing

Sow seed of summer radishes at fortnightly intervals from March to early June, 1 cm (½ in) deep in rows 15 cm (6 in) apart. Thin seedlings to 2.5 cm (1 in) apart. Sow winter radishes 1 cm (½ in) deep in rows 25 cm (10 in) apart in July or early August, thinning to 15 cm (6 in) apart.

Soil and site

A fertile, moisture-retentive soil is preferred, though summer radishes are not fussy. Spring sowings need a sunny site, summer ones require some shade.

Harvesting

Pull up summer radishes as soon as they are large enough. Winter radishes can be stored or left in the ground until needed; cover the crowns with straw or peat.

RHUBARB

CULTIVATION

Planting

Plant crowns from late autumn to early spring, setting them 2.5 cm (1 in) below the surface and spacing them at least 90 cm (3 ft) apart.

Soil and site

Water-retentive, preferably slightly acidic soil in a sunny, open site. The crowns should never be allowed to dry out as they will die. Mulching with compost or well-rotted manure will both feed the plants and promote moisture retention.

Harvesting

From April to July or August.

Expert tip

Do not eat the leaves as they contain oxalic acid, which is poisonous to humans. However, they can safely be put on the compost heap.

Rhubarb is very hardy and frost-resistant, but you will need to remember that it will take up a permanent space as it does not like to be moved once established.

You will need to prepare your soil about four weeks before planting, removing any stones and adding as much organic matter as possible. Do not be tempted to remove any stalks during the first season and cut only a few the second season in order to give the plant time to become established. Patience is the key with this plant.

Rhubarb can be forced by placing a bucket or similar container over the plant to exclude any light. The extra warmth and lack of light will encourage speedy growth and give more tender, sweeter stems.

SALSIFY AND SCORZONERA

Salsify is an old-fashioned vegetable that is not always easy to find in supermarkets. It is also known as the oyster plant and vegetable oyster because it has a mild, oyster-like flavour. It resembles a pale, slender parsnip and is worthy of a place in your vegetable plot as it is so easy to grow. Scorzonera is very similar in appearance, except that it has a black-skinned root. Salsify is biennial and scorzonera is perennial, but both have exactly the same cultivation requirements.

These plants are relatively trouble-free but the beds will need frequent weeding as fast-growing weeds can take over. Hand-weeding is best; if you use a hoe, take care not to touch the crowns. Water in dry weather and apply a mulch in summer to provide nutrients and retain moisture.

CULTIVATION

Sowing

In mid to late spring, sow seed thinly or in stations of 3 seeds at 15 cm (6 in) intervals in drills at least 30 cm (12 in) apart. Sow at a depth of 1 cm (½ in) and thin seedlings to 1 every 15 cm (6 in).

Soil and site

Deep, light soil and an open, sunny site. Dig the soil the autumn before but do not add any manure or compost as this will cause the roots to fork. Add a general fertilizer the week before sowing.

Harvesting

From October to February; mulch with straw in cold areas. If frost is coming, lift what you need and store in a cool place wrapped in paper. Harvest with care as the roots are easily damaged when lifted from frozen ground.

SHALLOTS

CULTIVATION

Planting

From midwinter to early spring, plant sets 15 cm (6 in) apart in rows with 30 cm (12 in) between them. Push them into the soil, leaving the tip just above the surface.

Soil and site

Loose, well-drained soil in an open, sunny spot.

Harvesting

Lift from early to late summer.

Expert tip

Make sure you wait for the leaves to yellow before lifting shallots and do it on a dry day. Leave in a warm, well-ventilated spot out of full sun to dry out for one week before using or storing. The best way to store shallots is in a mesh bag or plaited into strings and hung in a cool, dry place.

Shallots are best grown from sets (immature bulbs) rather than from seed as they mature faster and are less vulnerable to pests and diseases. Their cultivation requirements are similar to those of onions, but they differ in that their bulbs are divided up into individual cloves, much like those of garlic.

Once you have planted your sets you will need to make sure they are watered thoroughly in their early stages. They require less water once they mature. A light layer of mulch will not only help to keep the weeds at bay but will also assist the ground in retaining moisture.

Keep an eye out for sets lifted by frosts or birds and push them back into the soil; if birds are a continuing problem, put netting over the sets to deter them.

SPRING ONIONS

Spring onions are part of the allium genus (see page 28) and have a milder flavour than normal onions. They make an ideal crop for growing in containers if you are short of space, or they can be grown in between crops that develop more slowly. Although it is not essential, thinning out of spring onions will produce a larger bulb.

Make sure the soil is well dug and has been treated with manure the previous autumn. Do not plant spring onions on a bed that has been freshly manured. Also avoid planting in an area where the previous crop was a member of the onion family. Refer to your crop rotation chart to see where they should be positioned in your vegetable plot.

Ensure that weeds are kept down as these will affect the quality of your crop. It is best to remove them by hand rather than with a hoe as spring onions hate having their roots disturbed.

CULTIVATION

Sowing

From March to July, sow outdoors 1 cm (½ in) deep in drills 10 cm (4 in) apart. Thin seedlings to 2.5 cm (1 in) apart. Sow in August for a crop from March to May the following year.

Soil and site

Open, rich, well-drained soil in a light, sunny position. Apply lime if your soil is acid.

Harvesting

From June to October or the following spring.

Expert tip

Repeat sowing every 2–3 weeks so that you have a continuous supply of spring onions for your salads.

SQUASH (SUMMER)

CULTIVATION

Sowing

Sow outdoors from late spring to early summer, 2 cm (1 in) deep and about 90 cm (3 ft) apart each way. Set 2 seeds at each station and thin out the weaker seedling. Putting cloches or jam jars over the seeds provides warmth and keeps mice away. Seeds can also be sown indoors, 1 per pot, in late April; harden off before planting out in June.

Soil

Well-manured, well-drained soil in a sunny position.

Harvesting

From July to October.

Expert tip

Like cucumbers, squash are cucurbits and they are affected by cucumber mosaic virus. Look for disease-resistant varieties.

Squashes are among the easiest vegetables to cultivate, so they are perfect for the gardener who is new to vegetable-growing. Summer squashes have much thinner skins than their winter relatives and are quicker to mature; some varieties can be harvested only 50 days after planting. Some have a compact bush habit, while the vines of the trailing varieties spread only 1–1.2 m (3¼–4 ft) so will not take up much room. Types of summer squash include courgette, marrow and patty pan squash.

Keep squash well watered as the fruits need plenty of moisture to form, watering around them rather than over them. Once the fruits start to swell, feed fortnightly with tomato fertilizer. Pick courgettes regularly to keep them cropping.

SQUASH (WINTER)

Large, colourful winter squash and pumpkins are a wonderful blast of colour in any vegetable plot. Winter squash are the bigger and slower growing of this family of vegetables and their fruit can need 80–120 days of growth before they are ready to harvest.

They will need plenty of space on your plot as their vines can spread 0.9–4.6 m (3–15 ft). If they are planted too close to one another you risk problems with disease, so leave plenty of room, especially for larger varieties.

The winter squash family includes butternuts, acorns, hubbards, spaghetti, delicatas and pumpkins. Like summer squash, they are hungry plants needing a lot of feeding and watering. Restrict them to 2–3 fruits per plant, or just one if you want to grow giant pumpkins.

CULTIVATION

Sowing

Sow seeds outdoors in late May or early June, 2 per station 1.2 m (4 ft) apart with 1.2–2.4 m (4–8 ft) between rows. Remove the weaker seedling of each pair. Alternatively, sow indoors in mid-spring in individual pots and transplant after hardening off in June.

Soil and site

In a rich, acid to neutral soil in a warm, sunny spot.

Harvesting

Pumpkins in early autumn, winter squash from late summer when the rind is tough enough to withstand pressure from a fingernail.

Expert tip

As squash benefit from lots of compost, it is possible to grow them directly on your mature compost heap.

STRAWBERRIES

CULTIVATION

Planting

Plant rooted runners in autumn, pot-grown plants as soon as you buy them in spring and summer. Allow 45 cm (18 in) between plants and 1 m (3¼ ft) between rows.

Soil and site

Moisture-retentive, fertile soil, preferably slightly acid. Dig in manure before planting.

Harvest

From early summer to mid-autumn, depending on variety.

Expert tip

Growing strawberries through a layer of straw minimizes the growth of weeds, helps to warm the soil and keeps the fruit free of mud. Prepare the soil first to a fine tilth and build it up into a mound to encourage good drainage.

Strawberries are ideal for any type of vegetable plot as they can be grown in a wide range of soils from light sand to heavy clay and still give a bountiful supply of sweet fruit. The only condition they do not enjoy is poorly drained soil, which can lead to disease.

Although strawberry plants can produce fruit for up to five or six years, it is advisable to renew beds after two to three years as the yields will be reduced dramatically and you may find that diseases can occur.

Place a net over your strawberry plants to prevent birds and even squirrels having a nibble at the fruit. Make sure you pick ripe strawberries straight away so that they do not rot on the plant and place straw under the fruit to prevent it lying on the ground.

SWEDES

Swedes are ideal for growing on a vegetable plot. Although they are slow to grow, they are hardy and can be left in the ground over winter. They are a relatively trouble-free crop and your job is mainly to make sure they are kept free of weeds and water them in dry spells to avoid woodier roots and the split skins that can occur when rain returns. However, if you see drooping leaves and distorted roots, this indicates that your swedes are suffering from club root, a typical problem with brassicas. Remove and burn affected plants and consider disease-resistant varieties next year; although you can treat the soil to try to eradicate the micro-organism that causes club root, this is not always successful. Improving drainage and liming the soil may help.

CULTIVATION

Sowing

In late spring and early summer, sow seeds thinly 1.5 cm (¾ in) deep in rows 38–45 cm (15–18 in) apart. Thin seedlings to 25 cm (10 in) apart.

Soil and site

Swedes need light, humus-rich soil with a pH between 7.0 and 7.4 and a sheltered, sunny position.

Harvesting

Pull up as needed from early autumn. They can be left in the ground until spring, but to avoid the task of digging them out of frozen ground, lift by midwinter then store in a cool, frost-free shed.

Expert tip

Swedes do not like water-logged soil. If your soil is not free-draining, grow them on a ridge.

SWEET POTATOES

CULTIVATION

Planting

Buy slips (cuttings) from late April onwards and plant immediately in small pots of potting compost. Leave in a frost-free place with good light until early summer.

Transplanting

Harden off then plant out 30 cm (12 in) apart with 75 cm (2½ ft) between the rows.

Soil and site

They need a slightly acid, fertile, free-draining soil, ideally sandy. Give them the warmest position you can. Feed fortnightly with a high-potassium liquid feed.

Harvesting

Lift in mid-September when the leaves begin to die back. Leave in a warm room for a few days while the skins harden, then store in a cool, dry place.

Sweet potatoes are not a traditional British crop, but it is possible to grow them outdoors in milder areas and you can now buy a hardier variety suitable for UK growers. This is the best course, but if you want to grow some bought from a grocery store or supermarket, try to obtain organic ones as they will not have been given an anti-sprouting treatment. Put them in moist sand in a warm place, or partially submerge in a jar of water. When the sprouts are about 7.5 cm (3 in) long, remove them from the tubers and put into potting compost in a warm place to root.

If you do not have the free-draining soil sweet potatoes need, plant them in ridges 15–30 cm (6–12 in) high. You can grow them up a wigwam or other support or allow them to trail along the ground.

SWEETCORN

Sweetcorn is fairly easy to grow and will reward you with an abundance of sweet kernels if treated properly. Because it is pollinated by the wind it crops better if it is planted in a block of several rows to ensure even pollination. It is also necessary to give the plants adequate spacing as the ears will be greatly reduced or not form at all if the plants are overcrowded.

If you want a continuous supply of corn through the summer into autumn, stagger plantings a few weeks apart or choose varieties that mature at different times.

Sweetcorn plants are heavy feeders, so work in plenty of well-rotted manure or other organic matter. They will also appreciate a dressing of nitrogen when the plants are about knee high.

CULTIVATION

Sowing

Sow seeds outdoors in May, 2.5 cm (1 in) deep and 38 cm (15 in) apart in blocks. In colder areas, sow indoors at 15–18°C (60–65°F) in April and harden off before planting out in June.

Soil and site

Rich, fertile, slightly acid soil in full sun.

Harvesting

From midsummer to autumn if different varieties are planted. Test by piercing a kernel with your fingernail; if it releases a milky white liquid the cobs are ready to be harvested.

Expert tip

Planting corn in cool soil will set back seedlings, so it is advisable to wait until the soil temperature has reached 21–24°C (70–75°F).

TOMATOES

CULTIVATION

Sowing

Sow seeds indoors in trays of compost in spring, covering lightly with compost or vermiculite. Keep moist at about 18°C (65°F) When true leaves appear, prick out into individual 7.5 cm (3 in) pots. If you want only a few plants, sow 2–3 seeds per pot and remove the weaker seedlings.

Transplanting

After the last frosts in your area, harden off and plant out, 45 cm (18 in) apart with 75 cm (2½ ft) between rows.

Soil and site

Fertile, well-drained soil in a sunny, sheltered spot. Keep them well watered.

Harvesting

Pick from July to late September or early October. Covering with fleece will help the last of the fruits to ripen.

Tomatoes are not difficult to grow in the right conditions, especially if you choose the tumbler and bush varieties which need little care once planted out. Add manure to the soil the previous autumn and periodically feed the plants with potash, especially ones grown in a container. Make sure you keep your tomatoes watered, but do not allow the soil to become sodden otherwise the fruit will lose some of its flavour.

Cordon tomatoes will need tying to a support. After about four trusses of tomatoes have formed, 'stop' the plants by pinching out the growing tip of the main stem. Bush types do not require stopping.

Growbags are a convenient way to cultivate tomatoes. Plant three to a bag, then you need to do little else other than water them regularly.

TURNIPS

The modern trend with turnips is to grow hybrid varieties and smaller Japanese types as they are less woody than the traditional turnips and can even be grated and eaten raw in a salad. They are a very fast crop to grow and can be ready for harvesting just 5–8 weeks from sowing. Picking them small (about the size of a golf ball) means they are tender and have more flavour, a long way from the mundane roots used in stews. Successional sowing will ensure you a good supply of the right size. Water turnips in a dry spell to avoid a woody texture and splits in the roots.

Turnip tops can also be used as a green vegetable. Cut them in mid-spring when they are 12–15 cm (5–6 in) high, after which they will regrow to give you several more crops.

CULTIVATION

Sowing

Sow seeds thinly in drills, about 1 cm (½ in) deep in rows 30 cm (12 in) apart. Sow early varieties from March to June and maincrops from mid-July to mid-August. For an early start, you can sow in February under cloches. Thin earlies to 12 cm (5 in) apart, maincrops to 23 cm (9 in).

Soil and site

Rich, well-drained soil with neutral pH in a sunny spot. Lime the previous autumn if necessary.

Harvesting

Lift earlies from May to September and maincrops from mid-October onwards. They can stay in the ground until needed, but in cold, wet areas are best lifted in November and stored.

PART 4

IDEAS FOR COOKING YOUR PRODUCE

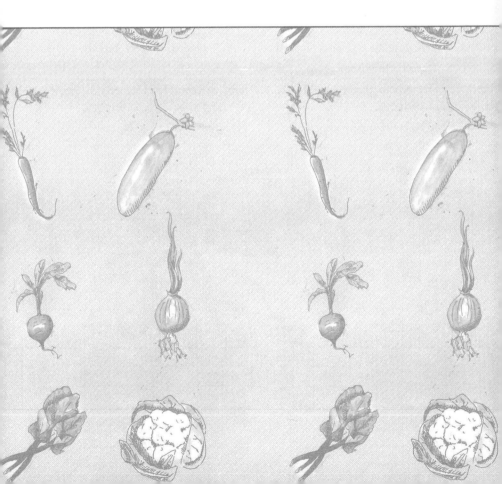

AUBERGINES
• • • • • • • • • • • • • • •

THAI CHILLI AUBERGINES

Serves 4

Preparation time: 10 minutes

Cooking time: 15 minutes

Ingredients

4 tbsp olive oil

4 garlic cloves, crushed and
   chopped

3 shallots, chopped

1 tbsp grated fresh root ginger

4 red chillies, chopped

4 cm (1½ in) lemongrass, crushed

2 aubergines, cut into 5mm (¼ in)
   slices

400 g (14 oz) can chopped
   tomatoes

juice of 1 lime

salt and freshly ground
   black pepper

Method

1. Heat the oil in a frying pan or wok and sauté the garlic, shallots, ginger, chillies and lemongrass for 2 minutes.

2. Add the aubergines, stir in and cook for 5 minutes.

3. Add the tomatoes and simmer for a further 5 minutes.

4. Season to taste with salt and pepper. Add the lime juice and cook for a further 3 minutes.

5. Serve in bowls, accompanied by steamed rice.

BROCCOLI
• • • • • • • • • • • •

SPICY PURPLE SPROUTING BROCCOLI WITH CHICKEN AND RED ONIONS

Serves 4

Preparation time: 10 minutes

Cooking time: 30 minutes

Ingredients

4 tbsp olive oil

4 chicken thighs

1 red onion, sliced

2 garlic cloves, crushed and
    chopped

1 tbsp grated fresh root ginger

2 red chillies, chopped

2 red peppers, cut into strips

2 spring onions, chopped

2 tbsp red curry paste

200 ml (7 fl oz) coconut milk

500 g (1 lb 2 oz) purple sprouting
    broccoli, cut into single stems

salt and freshly ground
    black pepper

about 2 tbsp light soy sauce

2 limes, cut into wedges

Method

1. Heat the oil in a frying pan or wok and brown the chicken thighs on both sides for about 5 minutes.

2. Remove the chicken and set aside. Sauté the red onion, garlic, ginger and chillies for 2 minutes.

3. Add the red peppers, spring onions and curry paste. Stir together and cook for about 4 minutes.

4. Add the coconut milk and simmer for a further 5 minutes.

5. Add the chicken and cook slowly for 8 minutes.

6. Add the broccoli and cook for another 2–3 minutes.

7. Season with salt, pepper and soy sauce to taste.

8. Add the juice from 1 lime and cook for another 3 minutes.

9. Reduce the heat to low for 1 minute to thicken the sauce.

10. Serve with boiled rice and lime wedges as a garnish.

CAULIFLOWER

CAULIFLOWER AND POTATO CURRY

Serves: 4
Preparation time: 10 minutes
Cooking time: 30 minutes

Ingredients

4 medium potatoes, chopped
1 medium cauliflower, chopped
4 tbsp olive oil
4 garlic cloves, crushed and
   chopped
1 red chilli, chopped
1 tbsp chopped fresh root ginger
1 onion, chopped
2 large tomatoes, chopped
2 tbsp curry powder of your
   choice (or make your own
   curry powder by mixing
   together ½ tsps paprika,
   turmeric, cumin, cinnamon
   and chilli flakes)
juice of 1 lime
salt and freshly ground
   black pepper

Method

1. Parboil the potatoes and cauliflower for 5 minutes and then drain.

2. Heat the oil in a frying pan or wok. Add the garlic, chilli, ginger and onion and brown together for 3 minutes.

3. Add the potatoes and cauliflower and stir together for about 2 minutes.

4. Add the tomatoes and curry powder and allow to cook for 8 minutes.

5. Add the lime juice and cook for another 5 minutes.

6. Add salt and pepper to taste and reduce the heat to low for the final 7 minutes.

7. Serve with boiled rice and warm naan bread.

COURGETTES
• • • • • • • • • • • • • • •

COURGETTE AND CLAM LINGUINE

Serves: 4
Preparation time: 10 minutes
Cooking time: 12 minutes

Ingredients

400 g (14 oz) linguine
600 g (1 lb 5 oz) clams
350 ml (12 fl oz) dry white wine
4 tbsp olive oil
4 shallots, chopped
2 garlic cloves, crushed and
   chopped
1 red chilli, chopped
4 courgettes, sliced
4 large tomatoes, chopped
2 tbsp chopped parsley
juice of 1 lemon
salt and freshly ground
   black pepper

Method

1. Cook the linguine in a pan of salted boiling water until al dente. Drain and set aside.
2. Wash the clams in cold water, then put in a saucepan. Dry heat the clams for 1 minute then add enough white wine to cover them. Boil for about 2 minutes until all the clams have opened. Remove from the heat, drain and reserve the wine as stock.
3. Heat the oil in a frying pan or wok, add the shallots, garlic and chilli and cook for 2 minutes.
4. Add the courgettes, tomatoes and half the reserved wine. Stir together for about 5 minutes.
5. Add the clams, 1 tablespoon of parsley and the linguine. Toss the mixture to thoroughly combine ingredients.
6. Add the remainder of the reserved wine and the lemon juice. Cook for a further 2 minutes.
7. Season to taste with salt and pepper and reduce the heat to low for 1 minute to thicken the sauce.
8. Serve sprinkled with black pepper and the remaining parsley as a garnish.

LEEKS
• • • • • • •

MONKFISH AND LEEK PIE

Serves 4

Preparation time: 10 minutes

Cooking time: 35 minutes

Ingredients

juice of 1 lemon

450 g (1 lb) monkfish tail, cut
   into chunks

3 leeks, cut into 1 cm (½ in) slices

450 g (1 lb) potatoes, peeled and
   roughly chopped

50 g (2 oz) butter

25 g (1 oz) plain flour

300 ml (½ pint) milk

salt and freshly ground
   black pepper

Method

1. Preheat the oven to 190°C
(375°F/Gas mark 5).

2. Squeeze lemon juice over
the monkfish.

3. Parboil the leeks in salted water
for 6–8 minutes. Drain thoroughly
and reserve the leek water.

4. Boil the potatoes in a pan
of salted water for 8 minutes.

5. While the potatoes are cooking,
make the sauce. Gently melt half
the butter in a small pan, sprinkle
in the flour and stir for 2 minutes
over a low heat. Remove from the
heat and very gradually stir in
all but 2 tablespoons of the milk.
Return to a low heat and cook,
stirring, until the sauce thickens.

6. Gradually add 150 ml (5 fl oz)
of the leek stock and bring back
to the boil, stirring constantly
to avoid lumps. Add salt and
pepper to taste. Remove from
heat when smooth and thick.

7. Drain the potatoes and add
the remaining butter and milk.
Mash together thoroughly. Season
with salt and pepper to taste.

8. Arrange the monkfish chunks
and leeks in an ovenproof dish.
Pour the white sauce over them
and cover with a layer of
mashed potato, fluffing up the
top with a fork.

9. Cook in the oven for 20
minutes or until the potato turns
golden brown.

ONIONS AND GARLIC

ONION SOUP WITH CHEESY BAGUETTES

Serves 4
Preparation time: 10 minutes
Cooking time: 35 minutes

Ingredients

50 g (2 oz) butter
4 onions, finely sliced
3 garlic cloves, minced
1 litre (1¾ pints) vegetable stock
2 glasses red wine
1 tsp grated nutmeg
1 tsp chopped fresh thyme
salt and freshly ground
    black pepper
8 slices white baguette
1 garlic clove, whole
50 g (2 oz) grated cheese
    (Gruyère or Cheddar)
4 tsp chopped fresh parsley

Method

1. Heat the butter in a frying pan and fry the onions gently until soft and translucent. Add the minced garlic during the last minute of cooking.

2. Pour in the vegetable stock and red wine and season to taste with nutmeg, thyme, salt and pepper. Bring to the boil and simmer for 30 minutes.

3. Toast the baguette slices and then rub a garlic clove over each one.

4. Check the soup for seasoning and ladle into ovenproof bowls. Float 2 slices of baguette on top of each bowl and sprinkle the grated cheese over the surface of both the baguette and the soup.

5. Place the bowls under a hot grill for a few minutes, or until the cheese has melted.

6. Serve with a sprinkling of chopped parsley.

PARSNIPS

The addition of honey and cinnamon in this recipe really brings out the flavour of the parsnips and makes them the perfect accompaniment for any meat.

PARSNIP PURÉE

Serves 4
Preparation time: 15 minutes
Cooking time: 30 minutes

Ingredients

900 g (1¾ lb) parsnips, cut into thick slices, woody centres of mature parsnips removed
50 g (2 oz) butter
1 egg yolk
1 tbsp honey
salt and freshly ground black pepper
1 tsp ground cinnamon
fresh parsley, to garnish

Method

1. Place the parsnips in a saucepan containing lightly salted boiling water. Cover and simmer for about 20 minutes or until tender.

3. Once the parsnips are cooked, drain them and mash into a purée. If you prefer you can put them in a food processor at this stage.

4. Return the parsnips to the saucepan, add the butter and beat with a fork until they are fluffy and heated through.

5. Beat in the egg yolk and honey and season to taste with salt, pepper and cinnamon.

6. Serve in a dish sprinkled with chopped parsley and a few extra sprigs of parsley for decoration.

POTATOES
• • • • • • • • • • • •

BULGARIAN POTATO PIE

Serves 4

Preparation time: 20 minutes

Cooking time: 1¼ hours

Ingredients

1 kg (2¼ lb) potatoes, peeled and
  cut into 12 mm (½ in) slices
6 tbsp groundnut olive oil
1 large onion, finely chopped
4 tbsp tomato purée
175 ml (6 fl oz) dry white wine
salt and freshly ground
  black pepper
1–2 tsp sweet paprika
2 tbsp white breadcrumbs

Method

1. Preheat the oven to 180°C
(350°F/Gas mark 4).

2. Rinse the potatoes under
cold water and pat dry, using
kitchen paper.

3. Heat 5 tablespoons of the oil
in a frying pan and fry the potato
slices for 2 minutes. Lift out using
a slotted spoon and drain on
kitchen paper.

4. Add the onion to the pan
and fry for 3 minutes. Stir in the
tomato purée and wine. Bring
to the boil and continue boiling
rapidly until the liquid has
reduced by one third.

5. Spoon half the potato slices
into a buttered ovenproof dish,
sprinkle with salt, pepper and
paprika to taste and then pour
half the sauce over them. Repeat
with the remaining potatoes
and sauce.

6. Top with the breadcrumbs
and drizzle the top with the last
tablespoon of oil. Cover with a lid
and bake in the lower half of the
oven for 1 hour.

7. Remove the lid for the last
15 minutes so that the top goes
brown and crispy.

RHUBARB
• • • • • • • • • • •

LIME MACKEREL WITH RHUBARB SAUCE

Serves 4
Preparation time: 5 minutes
Cooking time: 15 minutes

Ingredients

4 medium mackerel, cleaned,
    heads removed
juice of 2 limes
1 tsp grated fresh root ginger
salt and freshly ground
    black pepper
25 g (1 oz) butter
2 shallots, chopped
350 g (12 oz) fresh rhubarb, cut
    into chunks

Method

1. Make 3 diagonal cuts on each side of the mackerel and marinate them in a mixture of lime juice and ginger for 5 minutes.

2. Remove the mackerel from the marinade and season well with salt and pepper.

3. Melt the butter in a frying pan, add the shallots and fry gently for 5 minutes without allowing them to colour.

4. Add the rhubarb with a little of the marinade, and cook until it is tender.

5. Place some of the rhubarb mixture inside each mackerel and fry each fish gently for 5 minutes on each side.

6. Drizzle the sauce over the fish and serve them with a lime-garnished salad.

SQUASH AND PUMPKIN

SQUASH AND PUMPKIN SOUP

Serves 4
Preparation time: 20 minutes
Cooking time: 45–50 minutes

Ingredients

450 g (1 lb) pumpkin, flesh cut
  into chunks
450 g (1 lb) butternut squash, flesh
  cut into chunks
100 g (4 oz) butter
1 large onion, finely chopped
1 garlic clove, finely chopped
1 litre (1¾ pints) hot milk
salt and freshly ground
  black pepper
½ tsp cayenne pepper or to taste
1 tsp sugar
150 ml (5 fl oz) cream (optional)
finely chopped dill or chervil to
  garnish

Method

1. Put the pumpkin and squash
in a saucepan containing lightly
salted water. Bring to the boil and
simmer for about 15 minutes or
until they are soft.

2. Drain the pumpkin and
squash and either rub through
a coarse sieve or put into a food
processor to make a purée.

3. Melt the butter in a frying pan
and add the onion and garlic.
Fry over a medium heat for
about 5 minutes until soft and
transparent.

4. Add the purée and heat
through gently for 10 minutes,
stirring frequently to stop it from
burning.

5. Gradually add the hot milk
and then season to taste with
salt, pepper, cayenne pepper
and sugar.

6. Strain the soup through a
sieve and then return it to the
pan to heat again. Adjust the
seasoning if necessary and
add the cream (if used) without
allowing the soup to boil.

7. To serve, pour into soup bowls
and sprinkle with dill or chervil.

RADISHES

BRIE AND RADISH MOUSSE

Serves 4–6
Preparation time: 20 minutes
Chilling time: 3–4 hours

Ingredients

250 g (8 oz) ripe Brie, at room
    temperature
300 ml (½ pint) double cream
celery salt and white pepper to
    taste
20 g (¾ oz) powdered gelatine
14–16 radishes, trimmed and
    roughly chopped

Method

1. Make sure your Brie has been
out of the fridge for at least 1
hour. Remove and discard the
rind and place the Brie in a
bowl. Stir it with half the cream
until it is smooth. Season to
taste with celery salt and
white pepper.
2. Whisk the remaining cream
until it is fairly stiff and gradually
fold it into the cheese mixture.

3. Dissolve the gelatine in a little
water and blend thoroughly into
the creamed mixture.
4. Mix the radishes into the
cheese mixture.
5. Spoon the mousse into a
lightly oiled mould or dish. Chill
in the refrigerator for 3–4 hours or
until set.

GARNISH

If you really want to impress
your dinner guests you can
make some attractive radish
garnishes to decorate the
mousse. To make radish roses,
choose radishes that are round.
Trim off the roots and make
6–8 cuts lengthways from the
root end towards the stalk. Place
the radishes in a bowl of iced
water with a few ice cubes, and
leave in the refrigerator until
the cuts start to open out just like
flower petals.

STRAWBERRIES
• • • • • • • • • • • • • • • •

STRAWBERRY TRIFLE

Serves 4–6

Preparation time: 25 minutes

Cooking time: 20 minutes

Ingredients

100 g (4 oz) macaroons, roughly
   broken

2 tbsp sherry

450 g (1 lb) strawberries, hulled

1 tbsp caster sugar

3 egg yolks

50 g (2 oz) granulated sugar

300 ml (½ pint) single cream

½ vanilla pod

1 tsp cornflour, blended with
   1 tbsp cold milk

Method

1. Lay the macaroons over the
base of a glass dish. Pour the
sherry over them and leave
to soak.

2. While the macaroons are
soaking, rinse the strawberries
and drain on kitchen paper. Set
8–10 strawberries to one side to
use for decoration.

3. Cut the remaining strawberries
into small pieces and mash to a
rough purée. Stir in the caster
sugar and then spoon over the
top of the macaroons.

4. Beat the egg yolks with the
granulated sugar.

5. Put the cream and the vanilla
pod in a saucepan and bring to
the boil. Remove from the heat,
cover, and leave for 10 minutes.

6. Remove the vanilla pod and
gradually whisk the cream into
the egg yolks. Strain through a
sieve back into the pan and bring
back to just under boiling point,
whisking constantly to prevent
the custard from curdling.

7. Remove from the heat and stir
in the cornflour.

8. Once the custard is cool, pour
it over the top of the strawberries
and sprinkle with a little sugar
to prevent a skin from forming.
Chill before serving and top with
whole strawberries.

NETTLES
• • • • • • • • • •

NETTLE SOUP WITH PEARL BARLEY

Serves 4
Preparation time: 15 minutes
Cooking time: 25 minutes

Ingredients

about 250 nettles, only tips or very
    young leaves
50 g (2 oz) butter
1 large onion, finely chopped
1 large carrot, chopped
2 celery sticks, chopped
2 garlic cloves, crushed
1 litre (1¾ pints) vegetable stock
1 tsp freshly grated nutmeg
salt and freshly ground
    black pepper
50 g (2 oz) pearl barley, soaked in
    cold water overnight
2 tbsp thick cream or crème
    fraîche
juice of ½ lemon
chopped chives, to garnish

Method

1. Wearing rubber gloves and using scissors, cut off the tips from the nettles and wash them thoroughly. You only need to discard the tougher stalks, as the mixture will be liquidized later.

2. Melt the butter in a large frying pan and sweat the onion, carrot, celery and garlic until soft and translucent, but not brown.

3. Put the stock and nettles in a large saucepan and bring to the boil. Reduce the heat and simmer for about 5–10 minutes or until the nettles are tender.

4. Season with nutmeg, salt and pepper and once cool, slightly purée the soup in a liquidizer.

5. Cook the pearl barley in lightly salted water for 20–30 minutes or until tender.

6. Return the soup to a clean pan, stir in the cream or crème fraîche, lemon juice and pearl barley and reheat. Do not allow the soup to boil or it will curdle.

7. Check the seasoning and serve in individual bowls with a swirl of cream and a generous sprinkling of chopped chives.

GLOSSARY

Acidic With a pH balance below 7.
Alkaline With a pH balance above 7.
Allotment A plot of land, usually rented or leased for the purpose of growing fruit and / or vegetables.
Annual A plant that lives and dies in one growing season.
Anther The pollen-bearing part of a stamen.

Biennial A plant that takes two years to complete its growing cycle.
Biological control Using a natural organism to control a pest.
Blanching Keeping a crop in the dark to prevent bitterness and to achieve pale, tender shoots.
Bolting Premature flowering of a vegetable.
Brassica A member of the cabbage family.
Broadcast A technique for sowing seeds whereby seed is scattered over an area of ground rather than sown in rows.
Bud A shoot containing immature leaves or flowers.
Bulb A swollen underground bud formed from the plants leaves.

Capillary matting An absorbent mat that holds water.
Chitting Pre-sprouting by placing potatoes in a dark place.

Cloche A portable glass frame for protecting plants.
Compost A rich substance produced by the rotting down of plants.
Compost activator A mixture of micro-organisms and nutrients added to a compost pile to speed up the breakdown process.
Compound fertilizer A fertilizer that contains more than one plant nutrient.
Corm A swollen underground stem that resembles a bulb.
Curcubit A family of plants which includes marrow, courgette, melon, squash, gourd and pumpkin.
Cut-and-come-again A method of harvesting that allows more than one crop.
Cutting A section of plant that is removed and induced to sprout new growth.

Dibber A tool for making planting holes.
Divisions Sections of a perennial plant formed by dividing in more than one place.
Dormant Still alive but not actively growing.
Draw hoe A tool for making seed drills.

Earthing up Drawing up the soil around the stem of a plant.

Fertilizer A liquid or granular feed for flowers and vegetables.
Foliar feed Plant food sprayed directly on the leaves of a plant.
Forcing Placing plants in the dark to encourage pale and tender growth such as in rhubarb.

Garlic spray A solution of garlic, soap and water which acts as a deterrent to several types of insects.
Green manure Plants grown to cover the ground, then dug in to improve fertility.
Ground cover Plants that carpet the ground to suppress the growth of weeds.
Growbag Commercial sacks of compost for growing vegetables.

Hardening off Getting a plant used to outdoor conditions.
Hardiness A plant's resistance to low temperatures.
Heel-in To plant something temporarily into soil – often a trench – to await planting into its final position.
Herbaceous Plants that produce soft, woody growth that die down in winter and reappear in spring.
Horticultural fleece A lightweight synthetic fabric used to protect plants against frosts and pests.
Humus Organic residue of decayed vegetable matter.
Hybrid A variety of plant which has been selectively bred by a nursery or specialist breeder.

Insecticide A chemical used to destroy pests.
Irrigation A labour-saving technique for watering plants.

Leaf mould Decomposed leaves used as a compost.
Legumes Plants that belong to the pea and bean family.
Loam Fertile soil that contains a mixture of sand, clay, silt and organic matter.

Manure Organic animal and plant waste dug into the soil for its nutrients.
Mulch A layer of organic or inorganic matter placed on the soil to keep in moisture and to control weeds.

Nematode A microscopic soil-dwelling animal that is both parasitic and beneficial.

Organic Anything made from materials that have once been alive.
Organic matter Soil additives such as compost, leaf mould and farmyard manure.
Overwinter Keeping tender plants throughout the winter.

Perennial Plants that live for more than two years.
Pesticide A chemical used to kill pests.
Pinching out Removing the growing tip of the stem.
Plant out To transplant young

plants grown indoors to their outside position.

Pollination The fertilization of female parts of a flower by male pollen.

Potting The term used for putting plants in pots.

Potting on The term used for moving small seedlings into larger pots.

Propagator Covered seed trays used to encourage growth in controlled conditions.

Rhizome An underground stem that resembles a root.

Rootball A mass of roots and compost visible when a plant is pulled from the ground.

Rotation Moving groups of crops to a new position.

Rotivator A mechanical device for digging the ground.

Self-sow Seeds that have naturally distributed themselves from plants already growing.

Slow-release fertilizer A fertilizer that releases nutrients into the soil gradually.

Soil-less compost A growing compost that contains no loam.

Subsoil The infertile layer of soil just below the topsoil.

Sucker A shoot that grows from the base of the plant that can be removed and replanted.

Taproot A long, deeply penetrating root.

Tender A plant that cannot stand cold conditions.

Thinning out The process of removing seedlings to make more space.

Thrips Parasitic insects that feed on plants.

Tilth A soil that has been worked to a fine texture.

Topsoil A fertile top layer of soil.

Transpiration A process by which water is absorbed by the roots of a plant and evaporates through the leaves.

Truss A cluster of fruit at the end of a stem as in tomatoes.

Tuber An underground storage organ, such as a potato.

Tying in A method of holding climbers, tall perennials, fruit shrubs and bushes to a stake for support.

Variety A term used to describe a cultivated plant resulting from a controlled breeding or selection.

Windbreak A hedge, wall or fence that provides protection from strong winds.

Winter wash An insecticide or fungicide that is applied to plants during their dormant season.

INDEX